Linux for Beginners

and

I0009642

Command Line Kung Fu

JASON CANNON

Linux for Beginners

JASON CANNON

JASON CANNON

CONTENTS

INTRODUCTION

Knowing where to start when learning a new skill can be a challenge, especially when the topic seems so vast. There can be so much information available that you can't even decide where to start. Or worse, you start down the path of learning and quickly discover too many concepts, commands, and nuances that aren't explained. This kind of experience is frustrating and leaves you with more questions than answers.

Linux for Beginners doesn't make any assumptions about your background or knowledge of Linux. You need no prior knowledge to benefit from this book. You will be guided step by step using a logical and systematic approach. As new concepts, commands, or jargon are encountered they are explained in plain language, making it easy for anyone to understand.

Let's get started.

FIRST THINGS FIRST: GETTING ACCESS

In order to start learning your way around and putting your newfound knowledge to the test, you're going to need access to a Linux system. If you already have an account on a Linux system, you can skip ahead to the next chapter.

Web Based Command Line Access

The absolute quickest way to get access to a working Linux account is to visit http://www.simpleshell.com in your web browser and click "Start my session." A terminal emulator that is connected to a Linux server will be displayed. You will be automatically logged in using a generic account and presented with a shell prompt.

Since you do not have a personal account your shell history and any files that you create will be destroyed at the end of your session. SimpleShell is great for trying out a few commands or working for a short period of time since sessions are limited to 15 minutes each. You can easily start another session at the end of your 15 minutes, but just be aware that you will lose any work from the previous session.

Web Hosting Shell Accounts

If you use a web hosting service to host your website you may already have a Linux account that you can use. Consult your hosting company's documentation and search for "SSH" or "shell access." SSH stands for Secure Shell and it provides a way to connect to a server over a network, like the Internet. If you don't already have a web hosting provider, you can sign up for one and use it for shell access. Shared web hosting providers typically charge just a few dollars a month.

Here are some shared web hosting companies that can provide you with a shell account and SSH access.

- 1and1.com

- BlueHost.com

- DreamHost.com

- HostGator.com

- Site5.com

Using Preinstalled Linux Images

VirtualBox is virtualization software that can be installed on Windows, Mac, Solaris, or Linux. It allows you to run an operating system (guest) inside your current operating system (host). It's more time consuming than the other options, but it can be worth the extra effort to have your own personal Linux system. In this scenario you will spend a few minutes installing the virtualzation software, downloading a pre-installed Linux image, and importing that image.

To get started, head over to the VirtualBox download page located at https://www.virtualbox.org/wiki/Downloads and grab the installer for your current operating system. Click through the install screens and accept the defaults.

Next, download a virtual disk image (VDI) from http://virtualboxes.org to use. I recommend that you download a CentOS or Ubuntu image unless you already know which Linux distribution you will be working with in the future. Honestly, you can't make a wrong decision. The concepts that you will be learning in this book apply to any Linux distribution.

Launch VirtualBox, create a new virtual machine, and use the virtual disk image that you just downloaded. When you are asked for a hard disk image select the "Use existing hard disk" radio button and click on the directory icon. Next, click "Add" and select the virtual disk image. When the virtual machine is powered on you can log into the server using the username and password provided with the downloaded image.

Deep Dive

These links along with other supplemental material is available at:

http://www.linuxtrainingacademy.com/lfb

- How to Install VirtualBox on Mac - A video that guides you through the installation of VirtualBox on Mac. http://youtu.be/xBQdflx1L1o

- How to Install VirtualBox on Windows - A video that guides you through the installation of VirtualBox on Windows. http://youtu.be/CBhppdewtEQ

- VirtualBox Documentation - Official VirtualBox documentation https://www.virtualbox.org/wiki/Documentation

- VirtualBox download page - Where to obtain a copy of the VirtualBox software. https://www.virtualbox.org/wiki/Downloads

- VirtualBoxes.org - A good source of virtual disk images. http://virtualboxes.org/

GETTING CONNECTED

When your account is created you will be provided with details on how to connect to the Linux server. You may be provided with some or all of the following information:

- Username. This is also known as an account, login, or ID.

- Password

- SSH key

- Server name or IP address

- Port number

- Connection protocol

The connection protocol will either be SSH (Secure Shell) or telnet. SSH and telnet provide ways to connect to a server over the Internet or a local area network. In the vast majority of cases the connection protocol will be SSH. Telnet is practically obsolete at this point, however you may run into it if you need to access a legacy system.

Choosing an SSH Client

If you were given a specific SSH client to use, use that program and follow the documentation for that product. If you are free to choose your own client or were not provided one, I suggest using PuTTY for Windows or Terminal for Mac.

PuTTY can be downloaded from this website: http://www.LinuxTrainingAcademy.com/putty/. You only need putty.exe to get started.

The Terminal application comes pre-installed on Macs and is located in the /Applications/Utilities folder.

A list of other SSH clients is provided in the Deep Dive section at the end of this chapter.

Connecting via SSH with a Password from Windows

To connect to the Linux server using the SSH connection protocol, launch PuTTY.

Type the host name or IP address you were given into the Host Name (or IP address) box. If no port was given to you, leave it at the default value of 22.

Enter your username by clicking on `Data` in the left pane. It is located directly below `Connection`. Type your username into the `Auto-login username` field. If you skip this step you will be prompted for your username when you connect to the server.

Save your session by typing in a name in the `Saved Sessions` box and clicking `Save`. This allows you to speed up this process by simply double clicking on your saved session to connect to the Linux server.

When you click Open a connection attempt will be made. The first time you connect to a particular server, PuTTY will ask to cache that server's host key. You will not be prompted again on subsequent connections. To add the server's SSH host key to PuTTY's cache, simply click Yes when prompted.

Once you are successfully logged in, you will see something similar to this:

Connecting via SSH with a Password from Mac

The built-in SSH client on Mac is a command line program. Command line programs can be run with the Terminal application that comes with the Mac operating system. It is located in the /Applications/Utilities folder. The format of the ssh command is ssh -p port_number username@servername. If you were not provided a port number, then the default port of 22 is assumed and you can omit -p 22 from the ssh command. Similarly, the username only needs to be specified if it is different on the server than it is on your Mac workstation. For example, if your username on your Mac is bob and your username on linuxsvr is also bob, you can omit bob@ and simply type ssh linuxsvr. Once Terminal is running, type in the ssh command. Commands are case-sensitive and the ssh command is lowercase. It should look like one of these three options:

```
ssh linuxsvr
ssh bob@linuxsvr
ssh -p 2222 bob@linuxsvr
```

The first time you connect to a particular server you will be asked to verify that server's host key. You will not be prompted again on subsequent connections. When you are asked `Are you sure you want to continue connecting (yes/no)?` type `yes` and press `Enter`. Once you have established a connection, you will be prompted for your password.

```
air:~ bob$ ssh bob@linuxsvr
The authenticity of host 'linuxsvr (10.0.0.7)' can't be established.
RSA key fingerprint is cc:d8:f0:cf:c2:34:1a:69:80:7e:ad:c2:23:df:b9:4f.
Are you sure you want to continue connecting (yes/no)? yes
Warning: Permanently added 'linuxsvr,10.0.0.7' (RSA) to the list of known hosts.
bob@linuxsvr's password:
[bob@linuxsvr ~]$
```

Like Mac, Linux also comes with a terminal program and an SSH client. Once you are connected to one Linux server you can use the `ssh` command to connect to another Linux server. You can nest multiple connections and navigate through your network of Linux servers in this fashion.

General Information on Connecting via SSH with Keys

You may have not be given a password, but rather given an SSH key or even asked to generate one. In the physical world a key unlocks a door. Similarly, an SSH key is used to unlock the access to your account on a server. If you do not have a key, you cannot unlock the door.

Using account passwords or a combination of account passwords and SSH keys is a common practice. With the growth of cloud computing in recent years, it is becoming more and more popular to use SSH keys exclusively. Since cloud servers are often connected to the public internet, they are prone to brute force attacks. A mischievous person could write a program that repeatedly connects to your server trying a new username and password combination each time. They can increase their odds of gaining entry by using a list of common usernames and passwords. Configuring your cloud server to not accept account passwords and to only accept SSH keys eliminates this threat.

You can further increase the security of your SSH key by giving it a passphrase. In this case it takes something you have -- the key -- and something you know -- the passphrase -- to gain access to your account. If you feel confident that your key will only be under your control, you can forgo providing a passphrase for your key. This will allow you to log into servers without typing a password at all. Having an SSH key without a passphrase can allow you to automate and schedule tasks that require logging in to remote systems.

Importing SSH Keys on Windows

If you were given an SSH key that is not already in the PuTTY format, you will need to convert it. PuTTYgen is required in order to convert an SSH key on a Windows system.

Run PuTTYgen, click Load and navigate to the private SSH key you were given. The names of the files are typically id_rsa or id_dsa for private keys, and id_rsa.pub or id_dsa.pub for public keys.

Now you can save the public and private keys for later use with PuTTY.

Generating SSH Keys on Windows

In order to create an SSH key on a Windows system, you will need PuTTYgen.

When you run PuTTYgen you will be asked to move the mouse around to create some random data that will be used in the generation of the key.

You have the option to use a passphrase for your key. You can also change the comment to something more meaningful like Bob's key.

Now, save the public and private keys buy pressing Save public key and then Save private key. Give the public key to the system administrator so they can associate it with your account. The private key is for your eyes only. Do not share your private key!

Next, export the key as an OpenSSH key by clicking on `Conversions` and then `Export OpenSSH Key`. This OpenSSH key can later be used on Unix or Linux systems.

Connecting via SSH from Windows

Follow the "Connecting via SSH with a Password from Windows" instructions, but this time add one additional step to specify your SSH private key file. You can do this by by clicking on the plug sign (+) next to `SSH` in the left pane to reveal more options. Next click on `Auth`. In the right pane select `Browse` under the `Private key file for authentication` field and locate your private SSH key.

Generating SSH Keys on Mac

If you are asked to generate an SSH key, launch the Terminal application and use the command line utility named ssh-keygen. You will be asked a series of questions. Accept all the defaults by pressing Enter. Optionally enter a passphrase for your SSH key.

```
mac:~ bob$ ssh-keygen
Generating public/private rsa key pair.
Enter file in which to save the key
(/Users/bob/.ssh/id_rsa):
Enter passphrase (empty for no passphrase):
Enter same passphrase again:
```

```
Your identification has been saved in
/Users/bob/.ssh/id_rsa.
Your public key has been saved in
/Users/bob/.ssh/id_rsa.pub.
The key fingerprint is:
0b:14:c5:85:5f:55:77:35:5f:9e:15:a9:b4:b0:54:05
bob@mac
The key's randomart image is:
+--[ RSA 2048]----+
|        .o.o. .E+=@|
|        .o  o.. oO|
|        .  ...+ o.o|
|        .    .. o  |
|        . S        |
|         . .       |
|          .        |
|                   |
|                   |
+-----------------+
```

Connecting via SSH with Keys from Mac

If you generated your keys, this part is already done for you. If you were given an SSH key, you need to place it in a directory named .ssh underneath your home directory. Open the Terminal application and type in the following commands. Press the Enter key at the end of each line.

```
mkdir ~/.ssh
chmod 700 ~/.ssh
```

You will gain a full understanding of what these commands do as you progress through this book. In order to expedite the process of getting connected, the details will be saved for later.

Switch to the Finder to copy your keys into the .ssh folder. In the Finder menu click Go and then Go to Folder... and type ~/.ssh when prompted. When you click go, the .ssh folder will be displayed.

Now you can drag your keys into place.

Go to Folder

Go to the folder:

~/.ssh

Cancel   Go

Back in the Terminal window, set the proper permissions on your key files. (Again, these commands will be covered later.)

```
cd ~/.ssh
chmod 600 *
```

I highly recommend naming the keys in the following format: id_rsa and id_rsa.pub or id_dsa and id_dsa.pub Otherwise, you will have to specify the location of your key when you use the ssh command or perform some additional configuration to tell SSH that your keys are not named in the standard way.

As a general rule it makes your life much easier if you follow the standard conventions and common practices. I will point them out along the way. One of the things I love most about Linux is the freedom and power it gives you to do things in a myriad of ways. There are cases were not following the standard conventions will be the right thing to do.

If you still wish to name your key something else, you can tell SSH where to find it by adding -i key_location to the ssh command. Remember, the format of the ssh command we used above is ssh -p port_number username@servername. It can be expanded to ssh -i key_location -p port_number username@servername. Here's an example:

```
ssh -i /Users/bob/.ssh/bobs_key bob@linuxsvr
```

Connecting via Telnet

Telnet used to be the de facto way to connect to a Unix or Linux server. Over the years telnet has been replaced with Secure Shell, abbreviated SSH. SSH is, as its name implies, more secure than telnet. Telnet sends your login credentials over the network in plain text. SSH encrypts the communications between the client and the server, thus greatly improving security. If someone were to be packet snooping or eavesdropping on your connection, they would see garbled text and random characters. If you do have a need to telnet to a system you can use the SSH instructions from above, but with a couple of minor changes.

Connecting via Telnet from Windows

Run PuTTY and select the Telnet radio button. If no port was given to you, leave it at the default value of 23. You will be prompted for your username and password when you connect to the server.

Connecting via Telnet from Mac

The built-in telnet client on Mac is a command line program. Command line programs can be run with the `Terminal` application that comes with the Mac operating system. It is located in the `/Applications/Utilities` folder. The format of the telnet command is `telnet servername port_number`. You only need to include a port number if it is different than the default value of 23. You will be prompted for your username and password when you connect to the server.

```
mac:~ bob$ telnet linuxsvr
Trying 10.0.0.7...
Connected to 10.0.0.7.
Escape character is '^]'.
Ubuntu 12.04.3 LTS
linuxsvr login: bob
Password:
Last login: Thu Nov  7 01:26:37 UTC 2013
Welcome to Ubuntu 12.04.3 LTS

 * Documentation:  https://help.ubuntu.com/

  System info as of Nov 7 01:26:52 UTC 2013

  System load:  0.42
  Usage of /:   3.1% of 40GB
  Memory usage: 32%
  Swap usage:   0%
  Processes:           89
  Users logged in:     0
  IP address for eth0: 10.0.0.7

bob@linuxsvr:~$
```

Connecting Directly

If you are running Linux in VirtualBox as described in the previous chapter or you have dedicated hardware with Linux installed on it, you can simply log in directly to the server. You will be presented with a prompt requesting your username and password. If it is a graphical environment, you will need to find a terminal application to use after you have logged in. In most cases it will literally be "terminal", but you might see some slight variations like "gnome terminal", "konsole", or "xterm."

Here is what opening the terminal application looks like in CentOS. You will find it in one of the menus.

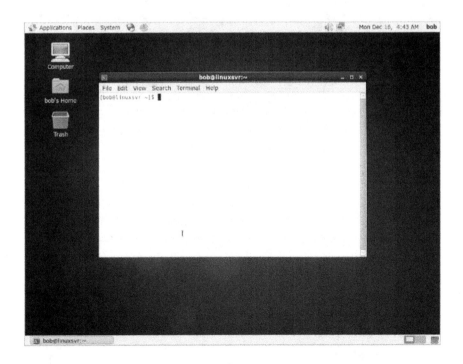

In some Linux graphical environments there may not be a traditional menuing system. In these cases you will want to search for the terminal application. In this Ubuntu example, click the button in the top left of the screen to bring up the dashboard. You can now start typing to find applications that are installed on the system.

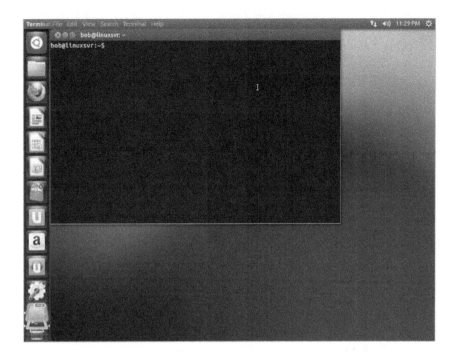

Deep Dive

- List of Mac SSH clients
  http://www.openssh.org/macos.html

- List of SSH clients, all platforms
  http://en.wikipedia.org/wiki/Comparison_of_SSH_clients

- List of Terminal Emulators - Includes terminals for Windows, Mac, and Linux.
  http://en.wikipedia.org/wiki/List_of_terminal_emulators

- List of Telnet Clients
  https://en.wikipedia.org/wiki/Telnet#Telnet_clients

- List of Windows SSH clients
  http://www.openssh.org/windows.html

- OpenSSH.org - The official website for OpenSSH.

- PuTTY
  http://www.LinuxTrainingAcademy.com/putty/

- Watch Star Wars over a telnet connection.

  - `telnet towel.blinkenlights.nl`

  - To disconnect, hold down the `Ctrl` key and press the right bracket (]). At the `telnet >` prompt type `quit` and press `Enter`.

- Using SSH Public Key Authentication
  http://macnugget.org/projects/publickeys

WELCOME TO SHELL

When you log into a server over the network the shell program is started and acts as your default interface to the system. The shell is nothing more than a program that accepts your commands and executes those commands. Said another way, the shell is a command line interpreter.

Let's look at the shell prompt you'll be working with. The prompt just sits and stares at you waiting for you do something interesting like give it a command to execute. Here is Bob's shell prompt.

```
bob@linuxsvr $
```

Bob's prompt is in a common format of `username@servername $`. In this example, the prompt is displaying the username, the server name, and if that user is using the system as a normal user ($) or a superuser (#).

The superuser on a Linux system is also called root. Anything that can be done on a server can be done by root. However, normal users can only do a subset of the things root can do. Root access is typically restricted to system administrators, but if you happen to support an application on a Linux server you may need root privileges to install, start, or stop it.

There are ways to grant specific users root privileges for specific cases. This is often accomplished with the `sudo` -- SuperUser Do -- program. That will be covered later. For now, just know that most of your day to day activities will be performed using a normal user account.

Your prompt might not look like Bob's. Common items that appear in prompts include the username, server name, present working directory, and the current time. Here are a few more prompt examples.

```
[bob@linuxsvr /tmp]$
linuxsvr:/home/bob>
bob@linuxsvr:~>
[16:45:51 linuxsvr ~]$
$
%
>
```

In two of the prompt examples you will notice a tilde (~). The tilde is a shorthand way of representing your home directory. In this example the tilde (~) is equivalent to `/home/bob`, which is Bob's home directory. This is called tilde expansion. A username can be specified after the tilde and it will be expanded to the given user's home directory. For example, `~mail` would expand to the home directory of the mail user which is `/var/spool/mail`. Another example is `~pat` expanding to `/home/pat`.

Prompts do not have to be contained on a single line. They can span multiple lines as in the following examples.

```
linuxsvr:[/home/bob]
$

(bob@linuxsvr)-(06:22pm-:-11/18)-]-
(~)

[Mon 13/11/18 18:22 EST][pts/0][x86_64]
<bob@linuxsvr:~>
zsh 14 %
```

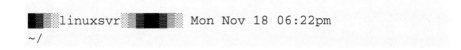

```
linuxsvr          Mon Nov 18 06:22pm
~/
```

For the remainder of this book the prompt will be shortened to the dollar sign ($) unless displaying the full prompt provides additional clarity. Also, the default prompt may vary from system to system, but you can customize it to your liking. That, along with other shell related topics, is covered in a later chapter.

Deep Dive

- Tilde Expasion
  http://gnu.org/software/bash/manual/html_node/Tilde-Expansion.html

LINUX DIRECTORY STRUCTURE

Now that you are able to connect to the server and have been introduced to the interface you will be using, it's time to learn about the directory layout. Understanding the directory structure will help you in the future when you are searching for components on the system. It can help you answer questions like:

Where are programs located?

Where do configuration files live?

Where might I find the log files for this application?

Common Directories

Here are the most common top level directories that you need to be aware of and may interact with as a normal user.

Dir	Description
/	The directory called "root." It is the starting point for the file system hierarchy. Note that this is not related to the root, or superuser, account.
/bin	Binaries and other executable programs.
/etc	System configuration files.
/home	Home directories.
/opt	Optional or third party software.
/tmp	Temporary space, typically cleared on reboot.
/usr	User related programs.
/var	Variable data, most notably log files.

Comprehensive Directory Listing

Here is a comprehensive list of top level directories that you may find on various Linux systems. Some subdirectories are included to help clearly define the purpose of the top level directory. You may never interact with many of these directories. Some of these directories will be on every system you encounter like /usr. Other directories are unique to specific Linux distributions. You can safely skim over this list and refer back to it if or when you have a practical need to do so.

Dir	Description
/	The directory called "root." It is the starting point for the file system hierarchy. Note that this is not related to the root, or superuser, account.
/bin	Binaries and other executable programs.
/boot	Files needed to boot the operating system.
/cdrom	Mount point for CD-ROMs.
/cgroup	Control Groups hierarchy.
/dev	Device files, typically controlled by the operating system and the system administrators.
/etc	System configuration files.
/export	Shared file systems. Most commonly found on Solaris systems.
/home	Home directories.
/lib	System Libraries.
/lib64	System Libraries, 64 bit.
/lost+found	Used by the file system to store recovered files after a file system check has been performed.
/media	Used to mount removable media like CD-ROMs.
/mnt	Used to mount external file systems.
/opt	Optional or third party software.

Dir	Description
/proc	Provides information about running processes.
/root	The home directory for the root account.
/sbin	System administration binaries.
/selinux	Used to display information about SELinux.
/srv	Contains data which is served by the system.
/srv/www	Web server files.
/srv/ftp	FTP files.
/sys	Used to display and sometimes configure the devices and busses known to the Linux kernel.
/tmp	Temporary space, typically cleared on reboot. This directory can be used by the OS and users alike.
/usr	User related programs, libraries, and documentation. The sub-directories in /usr relate to those described above and below.
/usr/bin	Binaries and other executable programs.
/usr/lib	Libraries.
/usr/local	Locally installed software that is not part of the base operating system.
/usr/sbin	System administration binaries.
/var	Variable data, most notably log files.

Dir	Description
`/var/log`	Log files.

Unix Specific Directories

Linux is often found in environments with other Unix variants. If you ever have a need to log into a Unix server you may see some of the following Unix specific directories.

Dir	Description
`/devices`	Device files, typically controlled by the operating system and the system administrators.
`/kernel`	Kernel and kernel modules. (Solaris)
`/platform`	Platform specific files. (Solaris)
`/rpool`	ZFS root pool directory. (Solaris)
`/net`	Used to mount external file systems. (HP-UX)
`/nfs4`	Used to mount the Federated File System domain root. (Solaris)
`/stand`	Files needed to boot HP-UX.

Note that you may encounter other top level directories that have not been listed above. However, those were most likely created by the system administrator.

Application Directory Structures

Applications can follow the same conventions employed by the operating system. Here is a sample directory structure of an application named apache installed in /usr/local.

Dir	Description
/usr/local/apache/bin	The application's binaries and other executable programs.
/usr/local/apache/etc	Configuration files for the application.
/usr/local/apache/lib	Application libraries.
/usr/local/apache/logs	Application log files.

Here is what it might look like if it was installed in /opt.

Dir	Description
/opt/apache/bin	The application's binaries and other executable programs.
/opt/apache/etc	Configuration files for the application.
/opt/apache/lib	Application libraries.
/opt/apache/logs	Application log files.

A common alternative to placing all the application subdirectories in /opt/app-name is to also use /etc/opt/app-name and /var/opt/app-name. Here is what that might look like for our example apache application.

Dir	Description
/etc/opt/apache	Configuration files for the application.
/opt/apache/bin	The application's binaries and other executable programs.
/opt/apache/lib	Application libraries.
/var/opt/apache	Application log files.

Sometimes applications that are not part of the standard operating system are installed in a shared manor and are not given their own subdirectory. For example, if apache was installed directly into /usr/local its binaries would live in /usr/local/bin and its configuration would live in /usr/local/etc. Apache may not be the only locally installed software so it would share that space with the other installed applications.

Another common practice is to create a directory structure based on a company, organization, or team name. For example, if you work at the Acme Corporation you may find a directory named /opt/acme or /usr/local/acme. Sometimes scripts and utilities are installed directly in that structure and other times there are segregated into their own subdirectories. Here's an example.

Dir	Description
/opt/acme	Company top level directory.
/opt/acme/bin	Binary programs created by or installed by the Acme Corporation.

Alternatively you may see something like this.

Dir	Description
`/opt/acme`	Company top level directory.
`/opt/acme/apache`	The top level directory for Acme's installation of apache.
`/opt/acme/apache/bin`	The apache binary programs.

Here are variations on the same idea, but based on a team within the company.

Dir	Description
`/opt/web-team`	The web support team's top level directory.
`/opt/acme/web-team`	The web support team's top level directory.
`/usr/local/acme/web-team`	The web support team's top level directory.

Example Top Level Directory Listings

Here is a listing of the top level directories for a few different Linux servers. Listing files and directories with the `ls` command will be covered in the next chapter.

Red Hat Enterprise Linux 6 (RHEL)

```
[bob@rhel6 ~]$ ls -1 /
bin
boot
cgroup
dev
etc
home
lib
lib64
lost+found
media
mnt
opt
proc
root
sbin
selinux
srv
sys
tmp
usr
var
```

SUSE Linux Enterprise Server 11 (SLES)

```
[bob@sles11 ~]$ ls -1 /
bin
boot
dev
etc
home
lib
lib64
lost+found
media
mnt
opt
proc
root
```

```
sbin
selinux
srv
sys
tmp
usr
```

Ubuntu 12.04 LTS

```
[bob@ubuntu12 ~]$ ls -1 /
bin
boot
dev
etc
home
lib
lib64
lost+found
media
mnt
opt
proc
root
run
sbin
selinux
srv
sys
tmp
usr
var
```

Deep Dive

- Filesystem Hierarchy Standard
  http://refspecs.linuxfoundation.org/FHS_2.3

- man hier

- RedHat Enterprise Linux
  http://redhat.com/products/enterprise-linux/

- SUSE Linux Enterprise Server
  https://www.suse.com/products/server/

- Ubuntu
  http://www.ubuntu.com/

BASIC LINUX COMMANDS

Here is a short list of basic, but essential commands. In Linux, commands are case-sensitive and more often than not they are entirely in lowercase. Items that are surrounded by brackets ([]) are optional. You will more than likely use at least some of these commands every time you log into a Linux system. Become familiar with these commands because they can get you pretty far in a short amount of time.

ls - Lists directory contents. You will use ls to display information about files and directories.

cd [dir] - Changes the current directory to dir. If you execute cd without specifying a directory, cd changes the current directory to your home directory. This is how you navigate around the system.

pwd - Displays the present working directory name. If you don't know what directory you are in, pwd will tell you.

cat [file] - Concatenates and displays files. This is the command you run to view the contents of a file.

echo [argument] - Displays arguments to the screen.

man command - Displays the online manual for command. Type q to quit viewing the manual page. The documentation provided by the man command is commonly called "man pages."

exit, logout, or Ctrl-d - Exits the shell or your current session.

clear - Clears the screen.

Here is a screen capture of Bob's session using the above commands.

```
$ ls
PerformanceReviews sales-lecture.mp3 sales.data
tpsreports
$ cd tpsreports
$ pwd
/home/bob/tpsreports
$ ls -l
total 2
-rw-r--r-- 1 bob users 31 Sep 28 14:49 coversheet.doc
-rw-r--r-- 1 bob users 35 Sep 27 08:47 sales-report
$ cat sales-report
We sold lots of widgets this week!
$ echo $PATH
/bin:/usr/bin:/usr/sbin:/usr/local/bin
$ man ls
NAME
       ls - list directory contents
...
```

More details on how you can fully exploit the power of these simple commands will be covered later. But right now, grab your fishing pole -- you're about to learn how to fish.

TEACH YOURSELF TO FISH

Knowing where executable commands live and the man command can take you a long way. You can teach yourself how to use Linux with this method, but it would be a long, slow process. More often than not, the man command will be used as a quick reference. It would be nearly impossible to memorize every option for every command and there is no need to do so when you have the man command at your fingertips.

To get help for the man command type the letter h while viewing a manual page. That will give you a list of commands you can use to navigate or search. Here is the concise version.

Enter - Move down one line.

Space - Move down one page.

g - Move to the top of the page.

G - Move to the bottom of the page.

q - Quit.

An environment variable is a storage location that has a name and a value. The one we are interested in at the moment is PATH. The PATH environment variable contains a list of directories that contain executable commands. You can determine the value of PATH by prepending it with a dollar sign ($PATH) and using the echo command to display its value to the screen.

```
$ echo $PATH
/bin:/usr/bin:/usr/sbin:/usr/local/bin
```

When you type in a command at the prompt and press Enter, that command will be searched for in the directories in your $PATH. In this example, /bin will be searched first. If the command is found it will be executed. If it is not found, then /usr/bin will be searched and so on. If no executable command is found that matches your request, you will be politely told that it cannot be found.

```
$ whatsupdoc
-bash: whatsupdoc: command not found
```

If you want to know exactly where a command is located you can use the which command. If the program cat is located in /usr/bin and in /usr/local/bin, the one which will get executed depends on your $PATH.

```
$ which cat
/bin/cat
$ which tac
/usr/bin/tac
```

Putting this all together, you can start looking at what is in each directory in your $PATH and use the man command to discover what each one of them does and how to use them. Remember, to exit the man command type the letter q.

```
$ echo $PATH
/bin:/usr/bin:/usr/sbin:/usr/local/bin
$ cd /bin
$ ls
awk diff cal cat cp date du echo grep groups less
more
```

```
$ man diff
NAME
      diff - compare two files
...
$ cd /usr/bin
$ ls
clear crontab cut dos2unix find kill mv pstree pwd
sed strings touch ...
$ man touch
```

Note that the output of the above ls commands was truncated. In reality there can be hundreds of commands in /bin and /usr/bin.

Many commands will provide hints for how to use them at the command line. Some commands will accept the -h flag, others will accept --help, and some will refuse to give you any help at all.

```
$ cal -h

Usage:
 cal [options] [[[day] month] year]

Options:
 -1, --one      show only current month (default)
 -3, --three    show previous, current and next month
 -s, --sunday   Sunday as first day of week
 -m, --monday   Monday as first day of week
 -j, --julian   output Julian dates
 -y, --year     show whole current year
 -V, --version  display version information and exit
 -h, --help     display this help text and exit
$ diff --help
Usage: diff [OPTION]... FILES
Compare files line by line.

  -i --ignore-case  Ignore case differences in file
contents.
  --ignore-file-name-case  Ignore case when comparing
file names.
...
```

If you are not sure what command to use, you can search through the man pages with `man -k KEYWORD`. From there you can read the man page for the command or ask it for help with `-h` or `--help`.

```
$ man -k calendar
cal         (1)   - display a calendar
zshcalsys   (1)   - zsh calendar system
```

Deep Dive

- ExplainShell - Type in a command-line to display help for each item.
  http://explainshell.com/

- Getting Help From Linux - An article from the Linux Journal on using man pages.
  www.linuxjournal.com/node/1022962

- LinuxManPages.com - This website allows you to search man pages or browse a category of commands and man pages.
  http://www.linuxmanpages.com/

- Linux commands broken down by category.
  http://linux.math.tifr.res.in/manuals/categories-index.html

WORKING WITH DIRECTORIES

Directories are simply containers for files and other directories. They provide a tree like structure for organizing the system. Directories can be accessed by their name and they can also be accessed using a couple of shortcuts. Linux uses the symbols . and .. to represent directories. Think of . as "this directory" and .. and "the parent directory."

Symbol	Description
.	This directory.
..	The parent directory.
/	Directory separator. Directories end in a forward slash and this is often assumed.

The directory separator is optional for the last subdirectory in a path or command. For example, the following commands work identically.

```
$ cd /var/tmp
$ cd /var/tmp/
```

Using the shortcuts can make navigating easier. For example, type cd.. to go to the directory just above your current directory.

```
$ pwd
/home/bob
$ cd tpsreports
$ pwd
/home/bob/tpsreports
$ cd ..
$ pwd
/home/bob
$ cd ..
$ pwd
/home
$ cd .
$ pwd
/home
```

The cd . command did not take you anywhere. Remember that . is "this directory" and .. is "the parent directory." Another shortcut for navigating directories is cd –. This command takes you to the previous directory. The environment variable that represents your previous working directory is OLDPWD. So, cd – and cd $OLDPWD are equivalent.

```
$ pwd
/home/bob
$ cd /var/tmp
$ pwd
/var/tmp
$ echo $OLDPWD
/home/bob
$ cd -
/home/bob
$
```

How would you execute a command that is in your current directory? Assume your current directory is your home directory. By default your home directory is not in your $PATH. Here is how to do that.

```
$ ./program
```

Why does that work? Well, . represents "this directory", / is the directory separator, and `program` is the program to execute. You can always use the full path to be explicit. Here are two ways to execute `program`.

```
$ pwd
/home/bob
$ ./program
$ /home/bob/program
```

Creating and Removing Directories

The `mkdir` command is used to create directories and the `rmdir` command removes them.

`mkdir [-p] directory` - Create a directory. Use the -p (parents) option to create intermediate directories.

`rmdir [-p] directory` - Remove a directory. Use the -p (parents) option to remove all the specified directories. `rmdir` only removes empty directories. To remove directories and their contents, use `rm`.

`rm -rf directory` - Recursively removes the directory and all files and directories in that directory structure. *Use with caution.* There is no "trash" container to quickly restore your file from when using the command line. When you delete something, it is gone.

```
$ mkdir newdir
$ mkdir newdir/product/reviews
mkdir: Failed to make directory
"newdir/product/reviews"; No such file or directory
$ mkdir -p newdir/product/reviews
$ rmdir newdir
rmdir: directory "newdir": Directory not empty
$ rm -rf newdir
$ ls newdir
ls: newdir: No such file or directory
$ pwd
/home/bob
$ cd ..
$ pwd
/home
```

LISTING FILES AND
UNDERSTANDING LS OUTPUT

Here is the output from an `ls` command using the `-l` option. The `-l` flag tells `ls` to display output in a long format. If you need to see what files or directories exist, use `ls`. However, if you need detailed information use `ls  -l`.

```
$ ls -l
-rw-rw-r-- 1 bob users 10400 Sep 27 08:52 sales.data
```

On the far left of the `ls` output is a series of characters that represent the file permissions. The number that follows the permissions represents the number of links to the file. The next bit of information is the owner of the file followed by the group name. Next the file size is displayed followed by the date and time when the file was last modified. Finally, the name of the file or directory is displayed. Here is the information displayed by the `ls  -l` command in table form.

Item	Value

Item	Value
Permissions	-rw-rw-r--
Number of links	1
Owner name	bob
Group name	users
Number of bytes in the file	10400
Last modification time	Sep 27 08:52
File name	sales.data

The meaning of `-rw-rw-r--` will be covered in detailed in the "File and Directory Permissions Explained" chapter.

Listing All Files, Including Hidden Files

Files or directories that begin with a period (`.`) are considered hidden and are not displayed by default. To show these hidden files and directories, use the `-a` option.

```
$ ls -a
.
..
.profile
.bash_history
lecture.mp3
PerfReviews
sales.data
tpsreports
```

Up until this point when you have used options, you have preceded each option with a hyphen (-). Examples are `-l` and `-a`. Options that do not take arguments can be combined. Only one hyphen is required followed by the options. If you want to show a long `ls` listing with hidden files you could run `ls -l -a` or `ls -la`. You can even change the order of the flags, so `ls -al` works too. They are all equivalent.

```
$ ls -l
total 2525
-rw-r--r--  1  bob   sales   25628  Sep 27  08:54  lecture.mp3
drwxr-xr-x  3  bob   users   512    Sep 28  09:20  PerfReviews
-rw-r--r--  1  bob   users   10400  Sep 27  08:52  sales.data
drwxr-xr-x  2  bob   users   512    Sep 28  14:49  tpsreports
$ ls -l -a
total 2532
drwxr-xr-x  4  bob   sales   512    Sep 28  14:56  .
drwxr-xr-x  14 root  root    512    Sep 27  08:43  ..
-rw-r--r--  1  bob   users   28     Sep 28  14:22  .profile
-rw-------  1  bob   users   3314   Sep 28  14:56  .bash_history
-rw-r--r--  1  bob   sales   25628  Sep 27  08:54  lecture.mp3
drwxr-xr-x  3  bob   users   512    Sep 28  09:20  PerfReviews
-rw-r--r--  1  bob   users   10400  Sep 27  08:52  sales.data
drwxr-xr-x  2  bob   users   512    Sep 28  14:49  tpsreports
$ ls -la
total 2532
drwxr-xr-x  4  bob   sales   512          Sep 28  14:56  .
drwxr-xr-x  14 root  root    512          Sep 27  08:43  ..
-rw-r--r--  1  bob   users   28           Sep 28  14:22  .profile
-rw-------  1  bob   users   3314         Sep 28  14:56
.bash_history
-rw-r--r--  1  bob   sales   25628  Sep 27  08:54  lecture.mp3
drwxr-xr-x  3  bob   users   512    Sep 28  09:20  PerfReviews
-rw-r--r--  1  bob   users   10400  Sep 27  08:52  sales.data
drwxr-xr-x  2  bob   users   512    Sep 28  14:49  tpsreports
$ ls -al
total 2532
drwxr-xr-x  4  bob   sales   512    Sep 28  14:56  .
drwxr-xr-x  14 root  root    512    Sep 27  08:43  ..
-rw-r--r--  1  bob   users   28     Sep 28  14:22  .profile
-rw-------  1  bob   users   3314   Sep 28  14:56  .bash_history
-rw-r--r--  1  bob   sales   25628  Sep 27  08:54  lecture.mp3
drwxr-xr-x  3  bob   users   512    Sep 28  09:20  PerfReviews
-rw-r--r--  1  bob   users   10400  Sep 27  08:52  sales.data
drwxr-xr-x  2  bob   users   512    Sep 28  14:49  tpsreports
```

Listing Files by Type

When you use the -F option for ls a character is appended to the file name that reveals what type it is.

```
$ ls
dir1 link program regFile
$ ls -F
dir1/ link@ program* regFile
$ ls -1F
total 8
drwxr-xr-x 2 bob users 117 Sep 28 15:31 dir1/
lrwxrwxrwx 1 bob users 7   Sep 28 15:32 link@ -> regFile
-rwxr-xr-x 1 bob users 10  Sep 28 15:31 program*
-rw-r--r-- 1 bob users 750 Sep 28 15:32 regFile
```

Symbol	Meaning
/	Directory.
@	Link. The file that follows the -> symbol is the target of the link.
*	Executable program.

A link is sometimes called a symlink, short for symbolic link. A link points to the location of the actual file or directory. You can operate on the link as if it were the actual file or directory. Symbolic links can be used to create shortcuts to long directory names. Another common use is to have a symlink point to the latest version of installed software as in this example.

```
bob@linuxsvr:~$ cd /opt/apache
bob@linuxsvr:/opt/apache ~$ ls -F
2.3/ 2.4/ current@
bob@linuxsvr:/opt/apache$ ls -l
drwxr-xr-x 2 root root 4096 Sep 14 12:21 2.3
drwxr-xr-x 2 root root 4096 Nov 27 15:43 2.4
lrwxrwxrwx 1 root root    5 Nov 27 15:43 current -> 2.4
```

Listing Files by Time and in Reverse Order

If you would like to sort the `ls` listing by time, use the `-t` option.

```
$ ls -t
tpsreports
PerfReviews
lecture.mp3
sales.data
$ ls -lt
total 2532
drwxr-xr-x 2 bob users 512      Sep 28 14:49 tpsreports
drwxr-xr-x 3 bob users 512      Sep 28 09:20 PerfReviews
-rw-r--r-- 1 bob sales 2562856 Sep 27 08:54 lecture.mp3
-rw-r--r-- 1 bob users 10400    Sep 27 08:52 sales.data
```

When you have a directory that contains many files it can be convenient to sort them by time, but in reverse order. This will put the latest modified files at the end of the `ls` output. The old files will scroll off the top of your display, but the most recent files will be right above your prompt.

```
$ ls -latr
total 2532
drwxr-xr-x 14 root root 512     Sep 27 08:43 ..
-rw-r--r-- 1 bob users 10400    Sep 27 08:52 sales.data
-rw-r--r-- 1 bob sales 256285   Sep 27 08:54 lecture.mp3
drwxr-xr-x 3 bob users 512      Sep 28 09:20 PerfReviews
-rw-r--r-- 1 bob users 28       Sep 28 14:22 .profile
drwxr-xr-x 2 bob users 512      Sep 28 14:49 tpsreports
drwxr-xr-x 4 bob sales 512      Sep 28 14:56 .
-rw------- 1 bob users 3340     Sep 28 15:04 .bash_history
```

Listing Files Recursively

Using the `-R` option with `ls` causes files and directories to be displayed recursively.

```
$ ls -R
.:
PerfReviews lecture.mp3 sales.data tpsreports
./PerfReviews:

Fred John old

./PerfReviews/old:
Jane.doc
$
```

You can also use the `tree` command for more visually appealing output. If you only want to see the directory structure, use `tree -d`.

`tree` - List contents of directories in a tree-like format.

`tree -d` - List directories only.

`tree -C` - Colorize output.

```
$ tree
.
├── PerfReviews
│   ├── Fred
│   ├── John
│   └── old
│       └── Jane.doc
├── sales.data
├── sales-lecture.mp3
└── tpsreports

2 directories, 6 files
$ tree -d
.
└── PerfReviews
    └── old

2 directories
$
```

List Directories, Not Contents

Normally when you run `ls` against a directory the contents of that directory are displayed. If you want to ensure you only get the directory name, use the –d option.

```
$ ls -l PerfReviews
total 3
-rw-r--r-- 1 bob users  36 Sep 27 08:49 Fred
-rw-r--r-- 1 bob users  36 Sep 28 09:21 John
drwxr-xr-x 2 bob users 512 Sep 27 12:40 old
$ ls -ld PerfReviews
drwxr-xr-x 3 bob users 512 Sep 28 09:20 PerfReviews
$ ls -d PerfReviews
PerfReviews
```

Listing Files with Color

Earlier you used `ls  -F` to help differentiate file types by adding a character to the end of their names in the `ls` output. You can also use color to distinguish file types by using `ls  --color`.

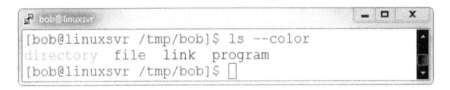

```
[bob@linuxsvr /tmp/bob]$ ls --color
directory  file  link  program
[bob@linuxsvr /tmp/bob]$ 
```

Commonly Used `ls` Options

Here is a recap of the `ls` options you have learned.

Option	Description
`-a`	All files, including hidden files
`--color`	List files with colorized output
`-d`	List directory names and not their contents
`-l`	Long format
`-r`	Reverse order
`-R`	List files recursively
`-t`	Sort by time, most recently modified first

Working with Spaces in Names

If you want to make your life easier when working from the command line, do not use spaces in file and directory names. Hyphens (-) or underscores (_) can be good substitutes for spaces. CamelCase, the practice of capitalizing each word, is another good option. For example, instead of naming your latest literary attempt "the next great american novel.txt" you could use "the-next-great-american-novel.txt", "the_next_great_american_novel.txt" or even "TheNextGreatAmericanNovel.txt."

Sooner or later you will encounter a file or directory that contains a space in the name. There are two ways to deal with this. The first is to use quotation marks. Even though the file name is a file, operate on it using "a file. " The second option is to escape the space. Escaping is like using quotes, but for single characters. The escape symbol is \, also known as a backslash. To escape a space, precede the space with the backslash (\) character.

```
$ ls -l
-rw-r--r-- 1 bob users 18 Oct 2 05:03 a file
$ ls -l a file
ls: a: No such file or directory
ls: file: No such file or directory
$ ls -l "a file"
-rw-r--r-- 1 bob users 18 Oct 2 05:03 a file
$ ls -l a\ file
-rw-r--r-- 1 bob users 18 Oct 2 05:03 a file
$ ls -lb a*
-rw-r--r-- 1 bob users 18 Oct 2 05:03 a\ file
$
```

The -b option to ls causes it to print escape codes. Note that quoting and escaping not only applies to spaces, but with other special characters as well including | & ' ; ( ) < > space tab.

Deep Dive

- Escaping Special Characters in Linux and Unix: With 7 Practical Examples - An article that takes a in-depth look at escaping. http://linuxg.net/escaping-special-characters-in-linux-and-unix-with-7-practical-examples/

- man bash - Look at the "QUOTING" section for handling special characters including spaces.

- man ls - To learn about all of the available options to ls refer to the man page.

FILE AND DIRECTORY PERMISSIONS EXPLAINED

Looking back at the long listings provided by the `ls` command you see that the first bit of information displayed is the permissions for the given file or directory.

```
$ ls -l sales.data
-rw-r--r-- 1 bob users 10400 Sep 27 08:52 sales.data
```

The first character in the permissions string reveals the type. For example, - is a regular file, `d` is a directory, and `l` is a symbolic link. Those are the most common types you will encounter. For a full listing read the `ls` man page.

Symbol	Type
-	Regular file
d	Directory
l	Symbolic link

You will also notice other characters in the permissions string. They represent the three main types of permissions which are read, write, and execute. Each one is represented by a single letter, also known as a symbol. Read is represented by r, write by w, and execute by x.

Symbol	Permission
r	Read
w	Write
x	Execute

Read, write, and execute are rather self explanatory. If you have read permissions you can see the contents of the file. If you have write permissions you can modify the file. If you have execute permissions you can run the file as a program. However, when these permissions are applied to directories they have a slightly different meaning than when they are applied to files.

Permission	File Meaning	Directory Meaning
Read	Allows a file to be read.	Allows file names in the directory to be read.
Write	Allows a file to be modified.	Allows entries to be modified within the directory.
Execute	Allows the execution of a file.	Allows access to contents and metadata for entries in the directory.

There are three categories of users that these permissions can be applied to. These categories or classes are user, group, and other. Like the permission types, each set is represented by a single letter. The user who owns the file is represented by u, the users that are in the file's group are represented by g, and the other users who do not own the file or are not in the file's group are represented by o. The character a represents all, meaning user, group, and other. Even though these characters do not show up in an ls listing, they can be used to change permissions.

Symbol	Category
u	User
g	Group
o	Other
a	All - user, group, and other.

Every user is a member of at least one group called their primary group. However, users can and often are members of many groups. Groups are used to organize users into logical sets. For example, if members of the sales team need access to some of the same files and directories they can be placed into the sales group.

Run the groups command to see what groups you are a member of. If you supply another users ID as an argument to the groups command you will see the list of groups to which that user belongs. You can also run id -Gn [user] to get the same result.

```
$ groups
users sales
$ id -Gn
users sales

$ groups pat
users projectx apache
$ groups jill
users sales manager
```

Secret Decoder Ring for Permissions

Now you have enough background information to start decoding the permissions string. The first character is the type. The next three characters represent the permissions available to the user, also known as the owner of the file. The next three characters represent the permissions available to the members of the file's group. The final three characters represent the permissions available to all others.

In this case order has meaning. Permission types will be displayed for user, followed by group, and finally for others. Also, the permission types of read, write, and execute are displayed in that order. If a particular permission is not granted a hyphen (–) will take its place.

Here is a graphical representation of the permission information displayed by `ls -l`.

```
Type   Group

-rw-r--r--  1 bob users 10400 Sep 27 08:52 sales.data

User   Other
```

If you happen to see an extra character at the end of the permissions string an alternative access control method has been applied. If you see a period (.), the file or directory has an SELinux (Security Enhanced Linux) security context applied to it. If you see a plus sign (+), ACLs (Access Control Lists) are in use. SELinux and ACLs are beyond the scope of this book. However, you will be pleased to know that the use of either of these is rare. If you are having troubles with permissions and notice an extra character in the permissions string, know that further investigation may be necessary.

```
$ ls -l sales.data.selnx
-rw-r--r--. 1 bob users 1040 Sep 27 08:52 sales.data.selnx
$ ls -l sales.data.acl
-rw-r--r--+ 1 bob users 1040 Sep 27 08:52 sales.data.acl
```

Changing Permissions

Permissions are also known as modes. That is why the command you use to change permissions is called chmod, short for "change mode." The format of the chmod command is chmod mode file. There are two ways to specify the mode. The first way is called symbolic mode. The symbolic mode format is chmod user_category operator permission. Here is a table view of the chmod command symbolic mode format.

Item	Meaning
chmod	The change mode command.
ugoa	The user category. One or more of u for user, g for group, o for other, a for all.
+-=	One of +, –, or =. Use + to add permissions, – to subtract them, or = to explicitly set them.
rwx	The permissions. One or more of r for read, w for write, and x for execute.

You can add, subtract, or set permissions using user category and permission pairs. For example, if you want to add the write permission for the members of a file's group, you would specify chmod g+w file.

```
$ ls -l sales.data
-rw-r--r-- 1 bob users 10400 Sep 27 08:52 sales.data
$ chmod g+w sales.data
$ ls -l sales.data
-rw-rw-r-- 1 bob users 10400 Sep 27 08:52 sales.data
```

Notice that after running chmod g+w sales.data the permissions string changed from '-rw-r--r--' to '-rw-rw-r--'. Remember that the permissions are displayed in the order of user, group, and other. The group permission set now includes the w symbol indicating that the write permission has been granted. Now the owner of the file (bob) and members of the group (users) can read and write to the sales.data file. Here is the reverse. This is how you would subtract the write permission.

```
$ ls -l sales.data
-rw-rw-r-- 1 bob users 10400 Sep 27 08:52 sales.data
$ chmod g-w sales.data
$ ls -l sales.data
-rw-r--r-- 1 bob users 10400 Sep 27 08:52 sales.data
```

You can change more than one permission at a time. This time write and execute permissions are added for the file's group.

```
$ ls -l sales.data
-rw-r--r-- 1 bob users 10400 Sep 27 08:52 sales.data
$ chmod g+wx sales.data
$ ls -l sales.data
-rw-rwxr-- 1 bob users 10400 Sep 27 08:52 sales.data
```

You can even set permissions on different user categories simultaneously. Here is how to change permissions for the user and group. Notice that before running this command that the user already has the write permissions. Using + to add permissions does not negate any existing permissions, it just adds to them.

```
$ ls -l sales.data
-rw-r--r-- 1 bob users 10400 Sep 27 08:52 sales.data
$ chmod ug+wx sales.data
$ ls -l sales.data
-rwxrwxr-- 1 bob users 10400 Sep 27 08:52 sales.data
```

If you want to set different permissions for different user categories, you can separate the specifications with a comma. You can mix and match to produce the outcome you desire. Here is how you can specify rwx for user while adding x for group.

```
$ ls -l sales.data
-rw-r--r-- 1 bob users 10400 Sep 27 08:52 sales.data
$ chmod u=rwx,g+x sales.data
$ ls -l sales.data
-rwxr-xr-- 1 bob users 10400 Sep 27 08:52 sales.data
```

If you want to set the file to be just readable by everyone, run chmod a=r file. When you use the equal sign (=) the permission are set to exactly what you specify. If you specify just read, then only read will be available regardless of any existing permissions.

```
$ ls -l sales.data
-rw-r--r-- 1 bob users 10400 Sep 27 08:52 sales.data
$ chmod a=r sales.data
$ ls -l sales.data
-r--r--r-- 1 bob users 10400 Sep 27 08:52 sales.data
```

If you do not specify permissions following the equal sign, the permissions are removed. Here is an illustration of this behaviour

```
$ ls -l sales.data
-rw-r--r-- 1 bob users 10400 Sep 27 08:52 sales.data
$ chmod u=rwx,g=rx,o= sales.data
$ ls -l sales.data
-rwxr-x--- 1 bob users 10400 Sep 27 08:52 sales.data
```

Numeric Based Permissions

In addition to symbolic mode, octal mode can be used with chmod to set file and directory permissions. Understanding the concepts behind symbolic mode will help you learn octal mode. However, once you learn octal mode you may find that it is even quicker and easier to use than symbolic mode. Since there are only a few common and practical permission modes they can be readily memorized and recalled.

In octal mode permissions are based in binary. Each permission type is treated as a bit that is either set to off (0) or on (1). In permissions, order has meaning. Permissions are always in read, write, and execute order. If r, w, and x are all set to off, the binary representation is 000. If they are all set to on, the binary representation is 111. To represent read and execute permissions while omitting write permissions, the binary number is 101.

r	w	x	
0	0	0	Binary Value for off
1	1	1	Binary Value for on
r	w	w	
0	0	0	Base 10 (decimal) value for off
4	2	1	Base 10 (decimal) value for on

To get a number that can be used with chmod, convert the binary representation into base 10 (decimal). The shortcut here is to remember that read equals 4, write equals 2, and execute equals 1. The permissions number is determined by adding up the values for each permission type. There are eight possible values from zero to seven, hence the name octal mode. This table demonstrates all eight of the possible permutations.

Octal	Binary	String	Description
0	000	---	No permissions
1	001	--x	Execute only
2	010	-w-	Write only
3	011	-wx	Write and execute (2 + 1)
4	100	r--	Read only
5	101	r-x	Read and execute (4 + 1)
6	110	rw-	Read and write (4 + 2)
7	111	rwx	Read, write, and execute (4+2+1)

Again, in permissions order has meaning. The user categories are always in user, group, and other order. Once you determine the octal value for each category you specify them in that order. For example, to get –rwxr-xr--, run chmod 754 file. That means the user (owner) of the file has read, write, and execute permission; the members of the file's group have read and execute permission; and others have read permissions

```
          U   G   O

Symbolic  rwx r-x r--

Binary    111 101 100

Decimal   7   5   4
```

Commonly Used Permissions

Here are the most commonly used permissions. These five permissions will let you do just about anything you need to permissions wise.

Symbolic	Octal	Use Case / Meaning
-rwx------	700	Ensures a file can only be read, edited, and executed by the owner. No others on the system have access.
-rwxr-xr-x	755	Allows everyone on the system to execute the file but only the owner can edit it.
-rw-rw-r--	664	Allows a group of people to modify the file and let others read it.
-rw-rw----	660	Allows a group of people to modify the file and not let others read it.
-rw-r--r--	644	Allows everyone on the system to read the file but only the owner can edit it.

When you encounter 777 or 666 permissions, ask yourself "Is there a better way to do this?" "Does everybody on the system need write access to this?" For example, if a script or program is set to 777, then anyone on the system can make changes to that script or program. Since the execute bit is set for everyone, that program can then be executed by anyone on system. If malicious code was inserted either on purpose or on accident it could cause unnecessary trouble. If multiple people need write access to a file consider using groups and limiting the access of others. It is good practice to avoid using 777 and 666 permission modes.

Working with Groups

If you work on the sales team and each member needs to update the sales.report file, you would set the group to sales using the chgrp command and then set the permissions to 664 (rw-rw-r--). You could even use 660 (rw-rw---) permissions if you want to make sure only members of the sales team can read the report. Technically 774 (rwxrwxr--) or 770 (rwxrwx---) permissions work also, but since sales.report is not an executable program it makes more sense to use 664 (rw-rw-r--) or 660 (rw-rw----).

When you create a file its group is set to your primary group. This behaviour can be overridden by using the newgrp command, but just keep in mind when you create a file it typically inherits your default group. In the following example Bob's primary group is users. Note that the format of the chgrp command is chgrp GROUP FILE.

```
$ nano sales.report
$ ls -l sales.report
-rw-r--r-- 1 bob users 6 Dec  4 20:41 sales.report
$ chgrp sales sales.report
$ ls -l sales.report
-rw-r--r-- 1 bob sales 6 Dec  4 20:41 sales.report
$ chmod 664 sales.report
$ ls -l sales.report
-rw-rw-r-- 1 bob sales 6 Dec  4 20:41 sales.report
```

Instead of keeping files in the home directories of various team members, it is easier to keep them in a location dedicated to the team. For example, you could ask the system administrator of the server to create a /usr/local/sales directory. The group should be set to sales and the permissions should be set to 775 (rwxrwxr-x) or 770 (rwxrwx---). Use 770 (rwxrwx---) if no one outside the sales team needs access to any files, directories, or programs located in /usr/local/sales.

```
$ ls -ld /usr/local/sales
drwxrwxr-x 2 root sales 4096 Dec  4 20:53
/usr/local/sales
$ mv sales.report /usr/local/sales/
$ ls -l /usr/local/sales
total 4
-rw-rw-r-- 1 bob sales 6 Dec  4 20:41 sales.report
```

Directory Permissions Revisited

This example demonstrates how permissions effect directories and their contents. A common problem is having proper permissions set on a file within a directory only to have the incorrect permissions on the directory itself. Not having the correct permissions on a directory can prevent the execution of the file, for example. If you are sure a file's permissions have been set correctly, look at the parent directory. Work your way towards the root of the directory tree by running ls -ld . in the current directory, moving up to the parent directory with cd .., and repeating those two steps until you find the problem.

```
$ ls -dl directory/
drwxr-xr-x 2 bob users 4096 Sep 29 22:02 directory/
$ ls -l directory/
total 0
-rwxr--r-- 1 bob users    0 Sep 29 22:02 testprog
$ chmod 400 directory
$ ls -dl directory/
dr-------- 2 bob users 4096 Sep 29 22:02 directory/
$ ls -l directory/
ls: cannot access directory/testprog: Permission
denied
total 0
-????????? ? ? ? ?               ? testprog
$ directory/testprog
-su: directory/testprog: Permission denied
$ chmod 500 directory/
$ ls -dl directory/
dr-x------ 2 bob users 4096 Sep 29 22:02 directory/
```

```
$ ls -l directory/
total 0
-rwxr--r-- 1 bob users 0    Sep 29 22:02 testprog
$ directory/testprog
This program ran successfully.
```

Default Permissions and the File Creation Mask

The file creation mask is what determines the permissions a file will be assigned upon its creation. The mask restricts or masks permissions, thus determining the ultimate permission a file or directory will be given. If no mask were present directories would be created with 777 (rwxrwxrwx) permissions and files would be created with 666 (rw-rw-rw-) permissions. The mask can and is typically set by the system administrator, but it can be overridden on a per account basis by including a umask statement in your personal initialization files.

umask [-S] [mode] - Sets the file creation mask to mode if specified. If mode is omitted, the current mode will be displayed. Using the -S argument allows umask to display or set the mode with symbolic notation.

The mode supplied to umask works in the opposite way as the mode given to chmod. When you supply 7 to chmod, that is interpreted to mean all permissions on or rwx. When you supply 7 to umask, that is interpreted to mean all permissions off or ---. Think of chmod as turning on, adding, or giving permissions. Think of umask as turning off, subtracting, or taking away permissions.

A quick way to estimate what a umask mode will do to the default permissions is to subtract the octal umask mode from 777 in the case of directories and 666 in the case of files. Here is an example of a umask 022 which is typically the default umask used by Linux distributions or set by system administrators.

```
                      Dir    File
Base Permission       777     666
Minus Umask          -022    -022
                     ----    ----
Creation Permission   755     644
```

Using a umask of 002 is ideal for working with members of your group. You will see that when files or directories are created the permissions allow members of the group to manipulate those files and directories.

```
                      Dir    File
Base Permission       777     666
Minus Umask          -002    -002
                     ----    ----
Creation Permission   775     664
```

Here is another possible umask to use for working with members of your group. Use 007 so that no permissions are granted to users outside of the group.

```
                      Dir    File
Base Permission       777     666
Minus Umask          -007    -007
                     ----    ----
Creation Permission   770     660 *
```

Again, using this octal subtraction method is a good estimation. You can see that the method breaks down with the umask mode of 007. In reality, to get an accurate result each time you need to convert the octal permissions into binary values. From there you use a bitwise NOT operation on the umask mode and then perform a bitwise AND operation against that and the base permissions.

It is fine to gloss over the subtleties here since there are only a few practical umask modes to use. They are 022, 002, 077, and 007. Save yourself the binary math homework and look at the following table containing all the resulting permissions created by each one of the eight mask permutations.

Octal	Binary	Dir Perms	File Perms
0	000	rwx	rw-
1	001	rw-	rw-
2	010	r-x	r--
3	011	r--	r--
4	100	-wx	-w-
5	101	-w-	-w-
6	110	--x	---
7	111	---	---

Special Modes

Look at this output of umask when the mask is set to 022.

```
$ umask
0022
```

You will notice an extra leading 0. So far you have only been dealing with three characters that represent permissions for user, group, and other. There is a class of special modes. These modes are setuid, setgid, and sticky. Know that these special modes are declared by prepending a character to the octal mode that you normally use with umask or chmod. The important point here is to know that umask 0022 is the same as umask 022. Also, chmod 644 is the same as chmod 0644.

Even though special modes will not be covered in this book, here they are for your reference. There are links at the end of this chapter so you can learn more about these modes if you are so inclined.

setuid permission - Allows a process to run as the owner of the file, not the user executing it.

setgid permission - Allows a process to run with the group of the file, not of the group of the user executing it.

sticky bit - Prevents a user from deleting another user's files even if they would normally have permission to do so.

umask Examples

Here are two examples of the effects umask modes have on file and directory creation.

```
$ umask
0022
$ umask -S
u=rwx,g=rx,o=rx
$ mkdir a-dir
$ touch a-file
$ ls -1
total 4
drwxr-xr-x 2 bob users 4096 Dec  5 00:03 a-dir
-rw-r--r-- 1 bob users    0 Dec  5 00:03 a-file
$ rmdir a-dir
$ rm a-file
$ umask 007
$ umask
0007
$ umask -S
u=rwx,g=rwx,o=
$ mkdir a-dir
$ touch a-file
$ ls -1
total 4
drwxrwx--- 2 bob users 4096 Dec  5 00:04 a-dir
-rw-rw---- 1 bob users    0 Dec  5 00:04 a-file
```

Deep Dive

- Binary Number System - There are only 10 kinds of people in the world: those who understand binary and those who don't. http://mathsisfun.com/binary-number-system.html

- Every Possible Umask Mode - An article that lists every possible umask mode. http://linuxtrainingacademy.com/all-umasks

- Modes - Detailed permission information. https://en.wikipedia.org/wiki/Modes_(Unix)

- SELinux - The official SELinux project page. http://selinuxproject.org/

- Special File Permissions - An article describing setuid, setgid, and the sticky bit. http://docs.oracle.com/cd/E19683-01/806-4078/secfiles-69

- Ubuntu ACL Documentation – This applies not only to Ubuntu, but to other Linux distributions as well. http://help.ubuntu.com/community/FilePermissionsACLs

FINDING FILES

If you ever need to locate a file or directory you can use the `find` command. It can be used to find files by name, size, permissions, owner, modification time, and more.

`find [path...] [expression]` - Recursively finds files in path that match expression. If no arguments are supplied it find all files in the current directory.

```
$ find
.
./.profile
./.bash_history
./PerfReviews
./PerfReviews/Fred
./PerfReviews/current
./PerfReviews/current/tps-violations.log
./PerfReviews/John
./sales.data
. . .
```

Here are some useful ways in which to use the `find` command.

`find . -name pattern` - Displays files whose name matches pattern. This is case sensitive.

`find . -iname pattern` - Same as –name, but ignores case.

`find . -ls` - Performs an ls on each of the found files or directories.

`find . -mtime num_days` - Finds files that are num_days old.

`find . -size num` - Finds files that are of size num.

`find . -newer file` - Finds files that are newer than file.

`find . -exec command {} \;` - Run command against all the files that are found.

Let's look at some examples. Let's say you are looking for a file or directory named "apache." You think it is in /opt somewhere and are not quite sure if it is "Apache" or "apache." You could provide `find` with the path of `/opt`, use `-iname` to ignore case, and look for "apache."

```
$ find /opt -iname apache
/opt/web/Apache
```

To find all the files in /usr/local that end in "conf", you can use this command.

```
$ find /usr/local -name *conf
/usr/local/etc/dhcpd.conf
/usr/local/etc/httpd.conf
```

If you are looking for files that are more than 10 days old, but less than 13 days old in the current directory you can use this command.

```
$ find . -mtime +10 -mtime -13
./.profile
./PerfReviews
./PerfReviews/John
./tpsreports
./tpsreports/coversheet.doc
```

Find files that start with an "s" and perform an `ls` on them.

```
$ find . -name "s*" -ls
52  11 -rw-r--r-- 1 bob users 1040 Sep 27 08:52 ./sales.data
48   1 -rw-r--r-- 1 bob users   35 Sep 27 08:47 ./demos/sr.txt
53 112 -rw-r--r-- 1 bob sales  266 Sep 27 08:54 ./salesdemo.mp3
```

The `-size` argument to `find` takes a number followed by a letter that represents the unit of space. Valid options are:

c for bytes

k for Kilobytes (units of 1024 bytes)

M for Megabytes (units of 1048576 bytes)

G for Gigabytes (units of 1073741824 bytes)

Here is an example of how to find files that are larger than 300 megabytes.

```
$ find . -size +300M
./PerfReviews/current/tps-violations.log
```

Here is how to find directories that are newer than a given file. In this case you are looking for directories that are newer that "b.txt."

```
$ find . -type d -newer b.txt
./PerfReviews
./PerfReviews/current
./tpsreports
```

On some occasions you may want to run a command against a list of files. You can use the `find` command with the `-exec` option to do this sort of thing. Use a pair of braces (`{}`) to act as a placeholder for the current file being processed. The command is terminated with the semicolon (`;`) character. You need to either escape or quote the semicolon like this `' ; '` or like this `\;`. If you want to run the command `file FILE_NAME` on every file in the current directory you would use the following command.

```
$ find . -exec file {} \;
.: directory
./.profile: ASCII text
./.bash_history: ASCII text
./PerfReviews: directory
./PerfReviews/Fred: directory
./PerfReviews/current: directory
./PerfReviews/current/tps-violations.log: ASCII text
./PerformanceReviews/John: empty
./sales.data: data
```

As you can see `find` is a really powerful tool and it has even more features than you have seen so far. Take a look at the man page or refer to the links at this end of this chapter.

Locate - A fast find

Every time you run the `find` command it evaluates each file and returns the appropriate response. This can be a slow process at times. For instance, if you are looking for a file on the system and cannot narrow its location down to a subdirectory you would run `find / - name something`. That command looks at each and every file on the system. If you know the file's name or at least part of its name and just want to know where it resides, the `locate` command is the right tool for that job.

`locate pattern` - List files that match pattern.

Once a day all the files on the system are indexed by a process called `updatedb`. When you run `locate` it is simply querying the index or database created by `updatedb` and not looking at each file on the system. This is really, really fast. The down side is that the data is not in real time. If you are trying to find a file you created just a few minutes ago, chances are it is not yet indexed and `locate` will not find it. Also, `locate` can potentially return a file that matches your search, but the file may have removed from the system since the index was last updated. On some servers `locate` is not installed or enabled, so your only choice may be to use `find`.

Here is what it looks like when `locate` is disabled.

```
$ locate bob
locate: /var/locatedb: No such file or directory
```

If it is enabled you will get a quick response to your queries. Notice that you do not need to know the entire file name, just a portion works.

```
$ locate tpsrep
/home/bob/tpsreports
/home/bob/tpsreports/coversheet.doc
/home/bob/tpsreports/sales-report.txt
```

Deep Dive

- Find - Ubuntu documentation on the find command. https://help.ubuntu.com/community/find

- Locate - An article on the locate command. http://www.linfo.org/locate.html

- The /etc/passwd file - An article on the /etc/passwd file. http://www.linfo.org/etc_passwd.html

VIEWING AND EDITING FILES

Here are some simple commands that display the contents of files to the screen.

cat file - Display the entire contents of file.

more file - Browse through a text file. Press the Spacebar to advance to the next page. Press Enter to advance to the next line. Type q to quit viewing the file. Commands are based on the vi editor, which is covered in the next section.

less file - Like more but allows backward movement and pattern searches.

head file - Output the beginning (or top) portion of file.

tail file - Output the ending (or bottom) portion of file.

This is how you might examine a file named file.txt with the commands cat, tail, and more.

```
$ cat file.txt
This is the first line.
This is the second.
Here is some more interesting text.
Knock knock.
Who's there?
More filler text.
The quick brown fox jumps over the lazy dog.
The dog was rather impressed.
Roses are red,
Violets are blue,
All my base are belong to you.
Finally, the 12th and last line.
$ head file.txt
This is the first line.
This is the second.
Here is some more interesting text.
Knock knock.
Who's there?
More filler text.
The quick brown fox jumps over the lazy dog.
The dog was rather impressed.
Roses are red,
Violets are blue,
$ tail file.txt
Here is some more interesting text.
Knock knock.
Who's there?
More filler text.
The quick brown fox jumps over the lazy dog.
The dog was rather impressed.
Roses are red,
Violets are blue,
All my base are belong to you.
Finally, the 12th and last line.
$ more file.txt
Here is some more interesting text.
Knock knock.
Who's there?
...
```

By default `head` and `tail` only display ten lines. You can override this behavior and tell them to display a specified number of lines. The format is -n where n is the number of lines you want to display. If you only want to display the first line of a file use `head -1 file`. Want to display the last three lines? Then run `tail -3 file`.

```
$ head -2 file.txt
This is the first line.
This is the second.
$ tail -1 file.txt
Finally, the 12th and last line.
$
```

Viewing Files In Real Time

Using `cat` can be a fine way to view files that have fairly static content. However, if you are trying to keep up with changes that are being made in real time to a file, `cat` is not the best choice. A good example of files that can change often and rapidly are log files. For example, you may need to start a program and look at that program's log file to see what it is doing. For this case, use the `tail -f file` command.

`tail -f file` - Follow the file. Displays data as it is being written to the file.

```
$ tail -f /opt/app/var/log.txt
Oct 10 16:41:17 app: [ID 107833 user.info] Processing
request 7680687
Oct 10 16:42:28 app: [ID 107833 user.err] User pat
denied access to admin functions
. . .
```

Editing Files

Nano

If you need to edit a file right now and do not want to spend any time learning obscure editor commands, use nano. Nano is a clone of pico, so if for some reason the nano command is not available, pico probably is. It's not as powerful as some other editors, but it's definitely easier to learn.

When you start nano you will see the file's contents and a list of commands at the bottom of the screen. To run the commands, replace the caret symbol (^) with the Ctrl key. For example, to exit nano type Ctrl-x.

```
  GNU nano 2.0.6              File: file.txt

This is the first line.
This is the second.
Here is some more interesting text.
Knock knock.
Who's there?
More filler text.
The quick brown fox jumps over the lazy dog.
The dog was rather impressed.
Roses are red.
Violets are blue.
All my base are belong to you.
Finally, the 12th and last line.
                        [ Read 12 lines ]
^G Get Help   ^O WriteOut   ^R Read File ^Y Prev Page ^K Cut Text  ^C Cur Pos
^X Exit       ^J Justify    ^W Where Is  ^V Next Page ^U UnCut Text^T To Spell
```

Editing in nano is quite easy. The up and down arrow keys will take you to the previous or next lines as expected. The right and left arrow keys let you navigate forwards and backwards on the same line. Simply type the desired text into the editor. To save the file, type Ctrl-o. If you forget to save the file before you exit, nano will ask you if you want to save the file. To learn more type Ctrl-g for help.

Vi

While nano is great for simple edits, vi and emacs have more advanced and powerful features. There is a learning curve to using these editors as they are not exactly intuitive. It will require a bit of a time investment to become proficient. Let's start by looking at vi.

`vi [file]` - Edit file.

`vim [file]` - Same as `vi`, but with more features.

`view [file]` - Starts `vim` in read-only mode. Use `view` when you want to examine a file but not make any changes.

`Vim` stands for "Vi IMproved." It is compatible with the commands found in `vi`. Some of the additional features of `vim` include syntax highlighting, the ability to edit files over the network, multi-level undo/redo, and screen splitting. On many Linux distributions when you invoke `vi`, you are actually running `vim`.

One advantage of knowing `vi` is that `vi` or a `vi` variant like `vim` is always available on the system. Another advantage is that once you learn the key mappings for `vi` you can apply them to other commands like `man`, `more`, `less`, `view`, and even your shell.

Vi Modes

Command Mode

`Vi` has the concept of modes. You are always working in one of three modes: command mode, insert mode, or line mode. When `vi` starts you are placed into command mode. To get back to command mode at any time hit the escape key (`Esc`). Letters typed while in command mode are not sent to the file, but are rather interpreted as commands. Command mode allows you to navigate about the file, perform searches, delete text, copy text, and paste text.

Here are some commonly used key bindings for navigation.

`k` - Up one line.

`j` - Down one line.

h - Left one character.

l - Right one character.

w - Right one word.

b - Left one word.

^ - Go to the beginning of the line.

$ - Go to the end of the line.

Note that commands are case sensitive. For example, if you want to move down one line type the lowercase j. The uppercase J joins lines together. The original vi editor did not employ the use of arrow keys, however vim does, so you may find that you can use arrow keys on your system. The advantages of learning the original key bindings are 1) they always work and 2) it's faster since your hand does not have to leave the home row.

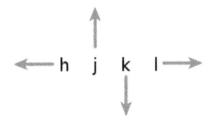

Insert mode

To enter insert mode, press one of the following keys.

i - Insert at the cursor position.

I - Insert at the beginning of the line.

a - Append after the cursor position.

A - Append at the end of the line.

After entering into insert mode, type the desired text. When you are finished, type Esc to return to command mode.

Line mode

To enter line mode you must start from command mode and then type a colon (:) character. If you are in insert mode, type Esc to get back to command mode and then type a colon for line mode. Here are some of the most common line mode commands you will want to know.

:w - Writes (saves) the file.

:w! - Forces the file to be saved even if the write permission is not set. This only works on files you own.

:q - Quit. This will only works if there have not been any modifications to the file.

:q! - Quit without saving changes made to the file.

:wq! - Write and quit. After modifying a file this command ensures it gets saved and closes vi.

:x - Same as :wq.

:n - Positions the cursor at line n. For example, :5 will place the cursor on the fifth line in the file.

:$ - Positions the cursor on the last line of the file.

:set nu - Turn on line numbering.

:set nonu - Turn off line numbering.

:help [subcommand] - Get help. If you want more information on the   `:w`   command   type   `:help`   `:w`.

Mode	Key	Description
Command	Esc	Used to navigate, search, and copy/paste text.
Insert	i I a A	Also called text mode. Allows text to be inserted in the file.
Line	:	Also called command-line mode. Save the file, quit vi, replace text, and perform some navigation.

Here is a screenshot of `vim`. Tildes (~) represent lines beyond the end of the file.

Advanced Editing with `vi`

You can repeat commands in `vi` by preceding them with a number. For instance, if you would like to move the cursor up 5 lines type `5k`. If you would like to insert a piece of text 80 times, type `80i` and start entering the text. Once you hit `Esc` to return to command mode the text you typed will be repeated 80 times. If you would like to make a line of asterisks, you could type `80i*Esc`. Can you start to see how `vi` is more powerful than an editor like `nano`?

Deleting Text

`x` - Delete a character.

`dw` - Delete a word. To delete five words, type `d5w`. The repeating concept in `vi` shows up in many places.

`dd` - Delete a line. To delete 3 lines, type `3dd`.

`D` - Delete from the current position to the end of the line.

Changing Text

`r` - Replace the current character.

`cw` - Change the current word.

`cc` - Change the current line.

`c$` - Change the text from the current position to the end of the line.

`C` - Same as `c$`.

`~` - Reverses the case of a character.

Copying and Pasting

`yy` - Yank (copy) the current line.

y<position> - Yank the <position>. For example, to yank a word type yw. To yank three words type y3w.

p - Paste the most recent deleted or yanked text.

Undo / Redo

u - Undo.

Ctrl-r - Redo.

Searching

/<pattern> - Start a forward search for <pattern>.

?<pattern> - Start a reverse search for <pattern>.

Emacs

Emacs is another powerful editor. Some people really find themselves drawn to vi while others thoroughly enjoy using emacs. It's a bit of a rivalry in the Linux world, actually. Experiment with emacs and vi to see which one works for you. You can't make a bad choice as they are both great editors.

emacs [file] - Edit file.

When reading emacs documentation know that C-<char> means to hold down the Ctrl key while pressing <char>. For example, C-h means to hold down the Ctrl key while pressing the h key. If you see C-h t, that means to hold down Ctrl key while pressing the h key, release the Ctrl key and then type the letter t.

When you see M-<char>, that means hold down the "meta" key, which is the Alt key, while pressing <char>. You can also substitute the Esc key for the Alt key. So M-f translates to holding down the Alt key and pressing f or pressing and releasing Esc followed by typing the f key. You may need to use Esc for the meta key since Alt may be intercepted by your terminal program, for instance. If you want to simplify things, always use Esc for the meta key as it will work in all situations.

Here are some helpful emacs commands.

C-h - Help.

C-x C-c - Exit. While holding down Ctrl press x, continue to hold down Ctrl and press c.

C-x C-s - Save the file.

C-h t - Emacs has a nice built-in tutorial.

C-h k <key> - Describe key. Use this to get help on a specific key command or key combination.

Navigating

C-p - Previous line.

C-n - Next line.

C-b - Backward one character.

C-f - Forward one character.

M-f - Forward one word.

M-b - Backward one word.

C-a - Go to the beginning of the line.

C-e - Go to the end of the line.

M-< - Go to the beginning of the file.

M-> - Go to the end of the file.

Deleting Text

C-d - Delete a character.

M-d - Delete a word.

Copying and Pasting

C-k - Kill (cut) the rest of the current line of text. To kill the entire line, position the cursor at the beginning of the line.

C-y - Yank (or paste) from the previously killed text.

C-x u - Undo. Keep repeating for multi-level undo.

Searching

C-s - Start a forward search. Type the text you are looking for. Press C-s again to move to the next occurrence. Press Enter when you are done searching.

C-r - Start a reverse search.

Repeating

Like vi, emacs provides a way to repeat a command.

C-u N <command> - Repeat <command> N times.

For instance, to kill three lines of text type Ctrl-U 3 Ctrl-k.

You have only scratched the surface with the `vi` and `emacs` editors. There is so much more to learn if you are interested. Both editors have features that include macros, global replace, and more. Entire books have been written on each of the these editors.

Graphical Editors

So far you have learned about command line editors that are appropriate to use when you connect to a server via ssh. However, if you are running Linux as a desktop operating system you might be interesting in some graphical text editors and word processors. Here are some for your consideration.

- `emacs` - Emacs has a graphical mode, too.

- `gedit` - The default text editor for the Gnome desktop environment.

- `gvim` - The graphical version of `vim`.

- `kedit` - The default text editor for the KDE desktop environment.

If you are looking for a MicroSoft Word replacement, consider AbiWord or LibreOffice. LibreOffice not only includes a word processor, but it is a complete office suite with a spreadsheet program, a database, and presentation software.

If you are looking for a source code editor to aid in computer programming, look at Geany, jEdit, or Kate. Sublime Text is another option. It is a commercial product that runs on Windows, Mac, and Linux.

Specifying a Default Editor

Some commands rely on the $EDITOR environment variable to tell them which program to use for editing. Since cron's primary purpose is to schedule jobs, it delegates the task of editing files to another program. The crontab -e command invokes the editor specified by the $EDITOR environment variable. You can set $EDITOR in your personal initialization files to ensure your favorite editor is used, be it nano, emacs, vi, or something else.

```
$ echo $EDITOR
vi
```

Deep Dive

- Emacs How To - An emacs tutorial.
  http://help.ubuntu.com/community/EmacsHowto

- Emacs built-in tutorial - Start `emacs` and type `Ctrl-h t`.

- The Beginner's Guide to Nano
  http://www.howtogeek.com/howto/42980/

- Vi tutorial
  https://www.washington.edu/computing/unix/vi.html

- `vimtutor` - Run `vimtutor` from the command line start the vim tutorial.

- Welcome Back to Shell - The commands `more` and `less` are called pagers because they allow you to page through a file. You will learn more about them in the "Welcome Back to Shell" chapter.

COMPARING FILES

If you want to compare two files and display the differences you can use `diff`, `sdiff`, or `vimdiff`.

`diff file1 file2` - Compare two files.

`sdiff file1 file2` - Compare two files side by side.

`vimdiff file1 file2` - Highlight the differences between two files in the `vim` editor.

```
$ cat secret
site: facebook.com
user: bob
pass: Abee!
$ cat secret.bak
site: facebook.com
user: bob
pass: bee
$ diff secret secret.bak
3c3
< pass: Abee!
---
> pass: bee
```

```
$ sdiff secret secret.bak
site: facebook.com      site: facebook.com
user: bob               user: bob
pass: Abee!           | pass: bee
```

In the diff output, the text following the less-than sign (<) belongs to the first file. The text following the greater-than sign (>) belongs to the second file. The first line of the diff output provides some additional information. The first number represents line numbers from the first file and the second number represent lines from the second file. The middle character separating the line numbers will be a c meaning change, a d meaning deletion, or an a meaning an addition. In this example the third line of the first file is changed from "pass: Abee!" to the text on the third line in the second file which is "pass: bee."

In the sdiff output the pipe (|) character means that the text differs in the files on that line. You will also see the less-than sign (<) meaning that line only exists in the first file. The greater-than sign (>) means that line only exists in the second file.

Here is a screenshot of vimdiff secret secret.bak demonstrating how the changes are highlighted using color.

DETERMINING A FILE'S TYPE

There are clues as to what a file might contain. For instance, some files will have extensions. If a file ends in .txt, it is probably a text file. If a file has execute permissions, it might be a program. An easy way to determine the type of a file is to run the file command against it.

file file - Display the file type.

```
$ file /etc/passwd
/etc/passwd: ASCII text
$ file *
bin: directory
bob.tar: POSIX tar archive
test.data: data
test.txt: ASCII English text
email-reports.sh: Bourne-Again shell script, ASCII
text executable
```

Searching for Text in ASCII Files

If you are looking for text within a file, use the `grep` command.

`grep pattern file` - Search for pattern in file.

`grep -v pattern file` - Invert match. Return lines from file that do not match pattern.

```
$ cat secret
site: facebook.com
user: bob
pass: Abee!
$ grep user secret
user: bob
$ grep o secret
site: facebook.com
user: bob
$ grep -v o secret
pass: Abee!
```

Here are some more common options to use with grep.

grep -i - Perform a search, ignoring case.

grep -c - Count the number of occurrences in a file.

grep -n - Precede output with line numbers from the file.

```
$ grep User secret
$ grep -i User secret
user: bob
$ grep -ci User secret
1
$ grep -ni User secret
2:user: bob
```

Searching For Text in Binary Files

If you run grep against a binary file, it will simply display whether or not that information was found in the file, but it will not display the surrounding text. To look at textual data within a binary file use the strings command.

strings file - Display printable strings in binary files.

```
$ grep -i john BlueTrain.mp3
Binary file BlueTrain.mp3 matches
$ strings BlueTrain.mp3 | grep -i john
John Coltrane
John Coltrane
$
```

Pipes

You will notice that two commands have been chained together with a vertical bar, also known as the pipe symbol. The pipe (|) means take the standard output from the preceding command and pass it as the standard input to the following command. If the first command displays error messages those will not be passed to the second command. Those error messages are called "standard error" output. You will learn how to manipulate standard error output in the "Redirection" chapter.

Also notice that in the first occurrence of the grep command the format of grep -i pattern file was used. In the second, the format of grep -i pattern was used. In the first format the input for grep came from file. In the second format the input for grep came from the preceding command via the pipe.

If you run strings BlueTrain.mp3 a lot of text will be displayed on the screen. Instead of letting that text pass you by, you can feed it to grep -i john using a pipe. The result, as you can see, is that 'John Coltrane' was found twice in the strings BlueTrain.mp3 output.

Pipes aren't limited to just two commands. You can keep chaining commands together until you get the desired result you are looking for. Let's feed the output from grep to head -1 to limit the output to just one line.

```
$ strings BlueTrain.mp3 | grep -i john | head -1
John Coltrane
$
```

Let's say you only want to display the second word of the above output. You can use the cut command to accomplish that goal.

cut [file] - Cut out selected portions of file. If file is omitted, use standard input.

cut -d delimiter - Use delimiter as the field separator.

cut -f N - Display the Nth field.

To extract 'Coltrane' from 'John Coltrane', use a space as the delimiter (-d ' ') and print the second field (-f 2). The space was quoted since spaces are typically ignored by the shell. Single quotes or double quotes work the same in this situation.

```
$ strings BlueTrain.mp3|grep -i john|head -1|cut -d ' ' -f2
Coltrane
$
```

You will find that there are many small commands that do just one thing well. Some examples are awk, cat, cut, fmt, join, less, more, nl, pr, sed, seq, sort, tr, and uniq. Let's take an example using some of those commands and chain them together with pipes.

The /etc/passwd file contains a list of accounts on the system and information about those accounts. In this example, the goal is to find all of the users named "bob" listed in the /etc/passwd file and print them in alphabetical order by username in a tabular format. Here is one way you could do that.

```
$ cd /etc
$ grep bob passwd
bob:x:1000:1000:Bob:/home/bob:/bin/bash
bobdjr:x:1001:1000:Robert
Downey:/home/bobdjr:/bin/bash
bobh:x:1002:1000:Bob Hope:/home/bobh:/bin/bash
bobs:x:1003:1000:Bob Saget:/home/bobs:/bin/bash
bobd:x:1004:1000:Bob Dylan:/home/bobd:/bin/bash
bobb:x:1005:1000:Bob Barker:/home/bobb:/bin/bash
$ grep bob passwd | cut -f1,5 -d:
bob:Bob
bobdjr:Robert Downey
bobh:Bob Hope
bobs:Bob Saget
bobd:Bob Dylan
bobb:Bob Barker
$ grep bob passwd | cut -f1,5 -d: | sort
bob:Bob
bobb:Bob Barker
bobd:Bob Dylan
bobdjr:Robert Downey
bobh:Bob Hope
bobs:Bob Saget
```

```
$ grep bob passwd | cut -f1,5 -d: | sort | sed 's/:/ /'
bob Bob
bobb Bob Barker
bobd Bob Dylan
bobdjr Robert Downey
bobh Bob Hope
bobs Bob Saget
$ grep bob passwd | cut -f1,5 -d: | sort | sed 's/:/ /' |column -t
bob       Bob
bobb      Bob      Barker
bobd      Bob      Dylan
bobdjr    Robert   Downey
bobh      Bob      Hope
bobs      Bob      Saget
```

The above example shows the step-by-step thought process of how to go from one set of output and pipe it as the input to the next command. If you need to perform this action often you could save the final command for later use. As you can see, this simple concept of piping makes Linux extremely powerful.

Pipe Output to a Pager

Another common use of pipes is to control how output is displayed to your screen. If a command produces a significant amount of output it can scroll off your screen before you have the chance to examine it. To control the output use a pager utility such as more or less. You've already used those commands directly on files, but keep in mind they can take redirected input too.

```
$ grep bob /etc/passwd | less
bob:x:1000:1000:Bob:/home/bob:/bin/bash
bobdjr:x:1001:1000:Robert
Downey:/home/bobdjr:/bin/bash
bobh:x:1002:1000:Bob Hope:/home/bobh:/bin/bash
bobb:x:1005:1000:Bob Barker:/home/bobb:/bin/bash
...
```

```
$ ls -l /usr/bin | less
total 62896
-rwxr-xr-x 1 root root  35264 Nov 19  2012 [
-rwxr-xr-x 1 root root     96 Sep 26 20:28 2to3-2.7
-rwxr-xr-x 1 root root     96 Sep 25 18:23 2to3-3.2
-rwxr-xr-x 1 root root  16224 Mar 18  2013 a2p
-rwxr-xr-x 1 root root  55336 Jul 12  2013 ab
....
$ ps -ef | more
UID    PID  PPID  C STIME TTY      TIME CMD
root     1     0  0 Jan08 ?    00:00:00 /sbin/init
root     2     0  0 Jan08 ?    00:00:00 [kthreadd]
root     3     2  0 Jan08 ?    00:00:01 [ksoftirqd/0]
root     6     2  0 Jan08 ?    00:00:00 [migration/0]
root     7     2  0 Jan08 ?    00:00:04 [watchdog/0]
...
$
```

DELETING, COPYING, MOVING, AND RENAMING FILES

Removing Files

Eventually you will get tired of all the old files you created just laying around, cluttering up your home directory, and taking up precious space. To delete them, use the `rm` command.

`rm file` - Remove file.

`rm -r directory` - Remove the directory and its contents recursively. If you want to remove a directory with `rm`, you have to supply the `-r` argument.

`rm -f file` - Force removal and never prompt for confirmation.

Search patterns can be used to delete multiple files at once. It's a good idea to double check what you are going to remove with `ls` before you execute `rm`.

```
$ ls s*
sales-lecture.mp3 sales.data secret secret.bak
$ rm s*
$ ls -d .*
. .. .profile .bash_history
```

```
$ rm .*
rm: cannot remove '.': Is a directory
rm: cannot remove '..': Is a directory
$ ls -d .*
.  ..
```

Note that `rm .*` will not remove . (this directory) and .. (the parent directory).

Copying Files

To copy files, use the `cp` command. If you want to create a copy of a file you can run `cp source_file destination_file`. You can also copy a file, or a series of files, to a directory by using `cp file(s) dir`.

`cp source_file destination_file` - Copy source_file to destination_file.

`cp source_file1 [source_fileN ...] destination_directory` - Copy source_files to destination_directory.

`cp -i source_file destination_file` - Run `cp` in interactive mode. If the destination_file exists, `cp` will prompt you before it overwrites the file.

`cp -r source_directory destination` - Copy source_directory recursively to destination. If destination exists, copy source_directory into destination, otherwise create destination with the contents of directory.

```
$ cp file1 file2
$ mkdir dir
$ cp file1 file2 dir/
$ ls dir
file1 file2
```

```
$ rm dir/*
$ cp file1 file2 dir
$ cp -i file1 file2
overwrite file2? (y/n [n]) n
not overwritten
$ cp -r dir dir2
$ ls dir2
file1 file2
$ cp dir dir3
cp: dir is a directory (not copied).
$ mkdir dir3
$ cp -r dir dir2 dir3
$ ls dir3
dir   dir2
$ tree dir3
dir3
├── dir
│   ├── file1
│   └── file2
└── dir2
    ├── file1
    └── file2
```

Moving and Renaming Files

The way to rename files or directories in Linux is to use the mv command. The mv command moves files from one location to another. This can be used to relocate files or directories and it can be used to rename them also.

mv source destination - Move files or directories. If destination is a directory, source will be moved into destination. Otherwise source will be renamed to destination.

mv -i source destination - Run mv in interactive mode. If the destination exists, mv will prompt you before it overwrites the file.

Look at the following examples. They should make it clear how the mv command behaves in various situations.

```
$ ls -F
dir/    dir2/  dir3/  file1   file2
$ mv dir firstdir
$ ls -F
dir2/       dir3/       file1       file2       firstdir/
$ mv file1 file1.renamed
$ ls -F
dir2/             dir3/             file1.renamed  file2
firstdir/
$ mv file1.renamed firstdir/
$ ls -F
dir2/     dir3/     file2     firstdir/
$ ls -F firstdir/
file1           file1.renamed   file2
$ cat firstdir/file1
This text started out in file1.
$ cat firstdir/file2
This text started out in file2.
$ mv firstdir/file1 firstdir/file2
$ cat firstdir/file2
This text started out in file1.
$ ls -F firstdir/
file1.renamed   file2
$ mv -i firstdir/file1.renamed firstdir/file2
overwrite firstdir/file2? (y/n [n]) n
not overwritten
$
```

In the above example, a directory was renamed with `mv dir firstdir`. Next, a file was renamed with `mv file file1.renamed`. Next `file1.renamed` was relocated to the firstdir directory with the `mv file1.renamed firstdir/` command. A file was overwritten with the `mv firstdir/file1 firstdir/file2` command. If you want to be prompted before a file is overwritten use the `-i` option.

SORTING DATA

You have already seen the `sort` command in use. In the simplest form it sorts lines of text alphabetically.

`sort file` - Sort text in file.

`sort -k F file` - Sort by key. The F following `-k` is the field number.

`sort -r file` - Sort in reverse order.

`sort -u file` - Sort text in file, removing duplicate lines.

```
$ cat more-secrets
tags: credentials
site: facebook.com
user: bob
pass: Abee!
tags: credentials
$ sort more-secrets
pass: Abee!
site: facebook.com
tags: credentials
tags: credentials
user: bob
$ sort -u more-secrets
pass: Abee!
site: facebook.com
tags: credentials
user: bob
$ sort -ru more-secrets
user: bob
tags: credentials
site: facebook.com
pass: Abee!
$ sort -u -k2 more-secrets
pass: Abee!
user: bob
tags: credentials
site: facebook.com
```

CREATING A COLLECTION OF FILES

If you want to bundle a group of files and/or directories together in an archive, you can use the `tar` command. You may want to create a copy or backup of a group of files. You may have several files you want to transfer at once or as a set. In these situations, `tar` can help.

`tar [-] c|x|t f tarfile [pattern]` - Create, extract or list contents of a tar archive using pattern, if supplied.

You will notice that tar does not require a hyphen (-) to precede its arguments. Traditionally the hyphen is excluded, but tar still works with it. If you see `tar cf file.tar` it is the same as `tar -cf file.tar`. Here is a look at some of the most commonly used tar options.

`c` - Create a tar archive.

`x` - Extract files from the archive.

`t` - Display the table of contents (list).

`v` - Causes `tar` to be verbose.

`f file` - The tar archive file to perform operations against.

In the following example tar is used to create (`tar cf tps.tar`) an archive, list the contents of the archive (`tar tf tps.tar`) and extract the contents (`tar xf tps.tar`).

```
$ tar cf tps.tar tpsreports/
$ tar tf tps.tar
tpsreports/
tpsreports/sales-report.txt
tpsreports/coversheet.doc
$ cd /tmp
$ tar xf /home/bob/tps.tar
$ ls tpsreports/
coversheet.doc sales-report.txt
$
```

If you would like to see the files that are getting placed into the archive or extracted from the archive, use -v to enable verbose mode.

```
$ tar cvf misc.tar sec* tpsreports
secret
secret.bak
tpsreports/
tpsreports/sales-report.txt
tpsreports/coversheet.doc
$ tar xvf /home/bob/misc.tar
secret
secret.bak
tpsreports/
tpsreports/sales-report.txt
tpsreports/coversheet.doc
```

COMPRESSING FILES TO SAVE SPACE

`gzip file` - Compress file. The resulting compressed file is named file.gz.

`gunzip file` - Uncompress files.

`gzcat` or `zcat` - Concatenates and prints compressed files.

You can use the command `du` to display how much space is used by a file.

`du` - Estimates file usage.

`du -k` - Display sizes in Kilobytes.

`du -h` - Display sizes in human readable format. For example, 1.2M, 3.7G, etc.

Here are a couple of quick examples that demonstrate how to compress and uncompress files.

```
$ du -k data
15360 data
$ gzip data
$ du -k data.gz
26 data.gz
$ ls data*
data.gz
$ gunzip data.gz
$ ls data*
data
$ du -k misc.tar
10 misc.tar
$ gzip misc.tar
$ du -k misc.tar*
misc.tar.gz
$
```

COMPRESSING ARCHIVES

In modern versions of the `tar` command `gzip` compression is built-in. If you want to create, extract, or list the contents of a compressed archive use the `-z` argument. As a matter of convention compressed tar files will end in either `.tar.gz` or `.tgz`. Here is how this looks.

```
$ tar zcf tps.tgz tpsreports
$ ls *.tgz
tps.tgz
$ tar ztf tps.tgz
tpsreports/
tpsreports/sales-report.txt
tpsreports/coversheet.doc
$
```

If you run across an older version of `tar` without gzip compression built-in, you can use pipes to create compressed archives. When a hyphen (–) is used in place of a file name that means to use standard output. Running the command `tar cf - pattern` will create an archive of "pattern" and send the output to standard output which is normally your screen. If you follow the command with a pipe that standard output will be used as the input for the next command following the pipe. To force gunzip to send its output to standard out, use the `-c` argument. With this in mind, here is how you can create, list, and extract a compressed archive using `tar`, `gzip`, and pipes.

```
$ tar cf - tpsreports | gzip > tps.tgz
$ ls *.tgz
tps.tgz
$ gunzip -c tps.tgz | tar tf -
tpsreports/
tpsreports/sales-report.txt
tpsreports/coversheet.doc
$ cd /tmp
$ gunzip -c /home/bob/tps.tgz | tar xf -
$ ls tpsreports/
coversheet.doc sales-report.txt
$
```

REDIRECTION

You have already learned how to redirect output from one command and send it as input to another one by using pipes. In the previous example you saw another way to redirect output using the greater-than (>) sign. Let's take a closer look at I/O (input/output) redirection.

There are three default types of input and output. They are standard input, standard output, and standard error. By default, standard input comes from the keyboard and standard output and standard error are displayed to the screen. Each one of these I/O types is given a file descriptor. File descriptors are just numbers that represent open files. For humans it is easier for us to reference files by name, but it is easier for computers to reference them by number.

You may be thinking, "my keyboard isn't a file, nor is my screen." On one level that is true, but on another level it is not. Linux represents practically everything as a file. This abstraction allows you to do powerful things like take the standard output of one command that would normally be displayed to your screen and use it as input to another command. It's easier to run `cat file.txt | sort` than it is to type the entire contents of `file.txt` as the input to the `sort` command.

To demonstrate this concept, run `sort`, type in some text, and press `Ctrl-d` on a blank line. Here is how that looks.

```
$ sort
dddd
a
ccc
bb
<<<< Type Ctrl-d here >>>>
a
bb
ccc
dddd
$ cat file.txt
dddd
a
ccc
bb
$ cat file.txt | sort
a
bb
ccc
dddd
$
```

I/O Name	Abbreviation	File Descriptor Number
standard input	stdin	0
standard output	stdout	1
standard error	stderr	2

Use the greater-than sign (>) to redirect output and the less-than sign (<) to redirect input. The explicit way of using redirection is to provide a file descriptor number, however if it is omitted then file descriptor 0 is assumed for input redirection and 1 for output redirection.

> - Redirects standard output to a file, overwriting (truncating) any existing contents of the file. If no file exists, it creates one.

>> - Redirects standard output to a file and appends to any existing contents. If no file exists, it creates one.

< - Redirects input from a file to the command preceding the less-than sign.

```
$ ls -lF /opt/apache
drwxr-xr-x 2 root root 4096 Sep 14 12:21 2.3
drwxr-xr-x 2 root root 4096 Nov 27 15:43 2.4
lrwxrwxrwx 1 root root    5 Nov 27 15:43 current -> 2.4
-rw-r--r-- 1 root root 1048 Sep 14 12:58 README
$ ls -lF /opt/apache > files.txt
$ cat files.txt
drwxr-xr-x 2 root root 4096 Sep 14 12:21 2.3
drwxr-xr-x 2 root root 4096 Nov 27 15:43 2.4
lrwxrwxrwx 1 root root    5 Nov 27 15:43 current -> 2.4
-rw-r--r-- 1 root root 1048 Sep 14 12:58 README
$ ls -lF /opt/apache >> files.txt
$ cat files.txt
drwxr-xr-x 2 root root 4096 Sep 14 12:21 2.3
drwxr-xr-x 2 root root 4096 Nov 27 15:43 2.4
lrwxrwxrwx 1 root root    5 Nov 27 15:43 current -> 2.4
-rw-r--r-- 1 root root 1048 Sep 14 12:58 README
drwxr-xr-x 2 root root 4096 Sep 14 12:21 2.3
drwxr-xr-x 2 root root 4096 Nov 27 15:43 2.4
lrwxrwxrwx 1 root root    5 Nov 27 15:43 current -> 2.4
-rw-r--r-- 1 root root 1048 Sep 14 12:58 README
$ sort < files.txt
-rw-r--r-- 1 root root 1048 Sep 14 12:58 README
-rw-r--r-- 1 root root 1048 Sep 14 12:58 README
drwxr-xr-x 2 root root 4096 Nov 27 15:43 2.3
drwxr-xr-x 2 root root 4096 Nov 27 15:43 2.3
drwxr-xr-x 2 root root 4096 Sep 14 12:21 2.4
drwxr-xr-x 2 root root 4096 Sep 14 12:21 2.4
lrwxrwxrwx 1 root root    5 Nov 27 15:43 current -> 2.4
lrwxrwxrwx 1 root root    5 Nov 27 15:43 current -> 2.4
```

In the above examples `ls -lF /opt/apache > files.txt` is the same as `ls -lF /opt/apache 1> files.txt`. Also, `sort < files.txt` is the same as `sort 0< files.txt`. Do not use a space between the file descriptor number and the redirection operator. The file descriptor must immediately precede the redirection operator, otherwise it will be interpreted as another item on the command line.

```
$ ls -lF /opt/apache 1 > files.txt
ls: 1: No such file or directory
$ ls -lF /opt/apache 1> files.txt
$ sort 0 < files.txt
sort: open failed: 0: No such file or directory
$ sort 0< files.txt
-rw-r--r-- 1 root root 1048 Sep 14 12:58 README
-rw-r--r-- 1 root root 1048 Sep 14 12:58 README
drwxr-xr-x 2 root root 4096 Nov 27 15:43 2.3
drwxr-xr-x 2 root root 4096 Nov 27 15:43 2.3
drwxr-xr-x 2 root root 4096 Sep 14 12:21 2.4
drwxr-xr-x 2 root root 4096 Sep 14 12:21 2.4
lrwxrwxrwx 1 root root    5 Nov 27 15:43 current -> 2.4
lrwxrwxrwx 1 root root    5 Nov 27 15:43 current -> 2.4
$
```

Input and output redirection can be combined. This example shows `files.txt` being redirected as input for the `sort` command. The output of the `sort` command is then redirected to the `sorted_files.txt` file.

```
$ sort < files.txt > sorted_files.txt
$ cat sorted_files.txt
-rw-r--r-- 1 root root 1048 Sep 14 12:58 README
-rw-r--r-- 1 root root 1048 Sep 14 12:58 README
drwxr-xr-x 2 root root 4096 Nov 27 15:43 2.3
drwxr-xr-x 2 root root 4096 Nov 27 15:43 2.3
drwxr-xr-x 2 root root 4096 Sep 14 12:21 2.4
drwxr-xr-x 2 root root 4096 Sep 14 12:21 2.4
lrwxrwxrwx 1 root root    5 Nov 27 15:43 current -> 2.4
lrwxrwxrwx 1 root root    5 Nov 27 15:43 current -> 2.4
```

Standard Error

When a program encounters an error it reports its findings to standard error. File descriptor 1 is for standard output, 2 is for standard error. Remember that file descriptor 1 is the default file descriptor for output redirection. This can mean that not all of the output generated by a program is captured by default. Here is an example.

```
$ ls here not-here
ls: not-here: No such file or directory
here
$ ls here not-here > out
ls: not-here: No such file or directory
$ cat out
here
$ ls here not-here 2> out.err
here

$ cat out.err
ls: not-here: No such file or directory
$ ls here not-here 1> out 2> out.err
$ cat out
here
$ cat out.err
ls: not-here: No such file or directory
$
```

You will notice that when using > the error message was displayed to the screen and not redirected to the out file. To redirect the error messages you had to explicitly specify file descriptor 2 with 2>. You can send standard output to one file while sending standard error to another file. You can use this to your advantage by having one file that contains known good output and another file that you can examine for errors.

If you want to capture both standard output and standard error, use 2>&1. Normally with redirection a file follows the redirection operator. If you want to use a file descriptor instead of a file name, use the ampersand (&) symbol. So instead of redirecting standard error to a file (2>out.err), redirect it to standard output (2>&1). If you omit &, 1 will be treated as a file named 1.

& - Used with redirection to signal that a file descriptor is being used instead of a file name.

2>&1 - Combine standard error and standard output.

2> file - Redirect standard error to a file.

```
$ ls here not-here > out.both 2>&1
$ cat out.both
ls: not-here: No such file or directory
here
$
```

The command, ls here not-here > out.both 2>&1 means "send the standard output of ls here not-here to file the named out.both and append standard error to standard output." Since standard error is redirected to standard output and standard output is redirected to out.both, all output will be written to out.both.

Null Device

>/dev/null - Redirect output to nowhere.

If you want to ignore output, you can send it to the null device, /dev/null. The null device is a special file that throws away whatever is fed to it. You may hear people refer to it as the bit bucket. If you do not want to see errors on your screen and you do not want to save them to a file, you can redirect them to /dev/null.

```
$ ls here not-here 2> /dev/null
here
$ ls here not-here > /dev/null 2>&1
$
```

Deep Dive

- File Descriptors http://en.wikipedia.org/wiki/File_descriptor

- Here Documents
  http://en.wikipedia.org/wiki/Here-document

- Null Device
  http://en.wikipedia.org/wiki//dev/null

- Redirection
  http://en.wikipedia.org/wiki/Redirection_(computing)

TRANSFERRING AND COPYING FILES

You already know how to copy files from one location to another on the same system using the cp command. But what if you want to copy files from your local workstation to a Linux server or between Linux servers? For that you can use SCP or SFTP.

SCP is secure copy and SFTP is SSH file transfer protocol. Sometimes SFTP is referred to as secure file transfer protocol. SCP and SFTP are both extensions of the secure shell (SSH) protocol. This means that if you have SSH key authentication configured for SSH, it will also work with SCP and SFTP.

In order to use SCP or SFTP you need a client. Mac and Linux come with scp and sftp command line utilities. If you are running Windows, you can use the PuTTY Secure Copy Client (pscp.exe) and the PuTTY Secure File Transfer client (psftp.exe) programs. Command line utilities aren't your only option. There are graphical clients for each platform as well. Some run on Windows, Linux, and Mac like FileZilla, while others only run on one platform like WinSCP for Windows.

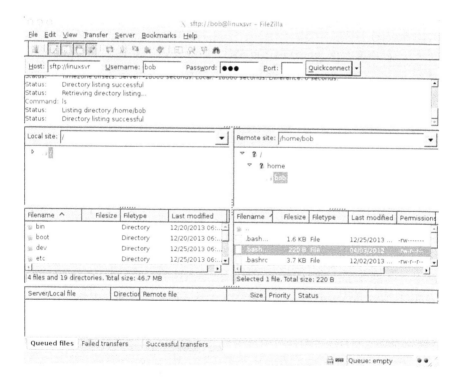

`scp source destination` - Copy source to destination.

`sftp [username@]host` - Connect to host as username to begin a secure file transfer session.

If you are looking for a more interactive experience where you can examine the local and remote file systems, use SFTP. With SCP you need to know what files you want to transfer before using the command. Here is a sample SFTP session.

```
bobby@laptop:/tmp $ sftp bob@linuxsvr
bob@linuxsvr's password:
Connected to linuxsvr.
sftp> pwd
Remote working directory: /home/bob
sftp> ls -la
drwxr-xr-x    4 bob   bob   4096 Dec 25 19:00 .
drwxr-xr-x    4 root  root  4096 Dec  2 22:01 ..
-rw-r--r--    1 bob   bob   3655 Dec  2 22:02 .bashrc
-rw-r--r--    1 bob   bob    675 Apr  3 2012 .profile
drwx------    2 bob   bob   4096 Dec 25 19:00 .ssh
sftp> lpwd
Local working directory: /tmp
sftp> lls
file1.txt
sftp> put file1.txt
Uploading file1.txt to /home/bob/file1.txt
file1.txt
100%    18      0.0KB/s    00:00
sftp> ls
file1.txt
sftp> ls -la
drwxr-xr-x    4 bob   bob   4096 Dec 25 19:02 .
drwxr-xr-x    4 root  root  4096 Dec  2 22:01 ..
-rw-r--r--    1 bob   bob   3655 Dec  2 22:02 .bashrc
-rw-r--r--    1 bob   bob    675 Apr  3 2012 .profile
drwx------    2 bob   bob   4096 Dec 25 19:00 .ssh
-rw-rw-r--    1 bob   bob     18 Dec 25 19:02 file1.txt
sftp> quit
```

Using `scp`, you can copy from your local system to a remote system, from a remote system to your local system, or from one remote system to another remote system. Here is how that looks.

```
$ scp test.txt linuxsvr1:~/
test.txt        100%    35KB   35.3KB/s    00:00
$ scp linuxsvr1:~/test.txt .
test.txt        100%    35KB   35.3KB/s    00:00
$ scp linuxsvr1:~/test.txt linuxsvr2:/tmp/test-copy.txt
$
```

SCP and SFTP aren't the only ways to transfer files to remote systems. Sometimes FTP (file transfer protocol) is enabled. In such cases you can use the built-in `ftp` command on Linux and Mac and a graphical client like WinSCP for windows. Just be aware that FTP is not using a secure transfer protocol like SCP and SFTP. This means that your login credentials are sent in plain text over the network. Also, the files that you upload and download are not encrypted either. If given the choice between SCP/SFTP or FTP, use SCP/SFTP.

```
bobby@laptop:~$ ftp linuxsvr
Connected to linuxsvr.
220 ubuntu FTP server (Version 6.4) ready.
Name (linuxsvr:bobby): bob
331 Password required for bob.
Password:
230 User bob logged in.
Remote system type is UNIX.
Using binary mode to transfer files.
ftp> pwd
257 "/home/bob" is current directory.
ftp> quit
221 Goodbye.
```

If FTP is not enabled, you will see a "Connection refused" error message.

```
bobby@laptop:~$ ftp linuxsvr
ftp: connect: Connection refused
ftp> quit
bobby@laptop:~$
```

Deep dive

- Connecting via SSH with Keys - SSH key information covered earlier in this book.

- Cyberduck - FTP and SFTP client for Mac and Windows. http://cyberduck.io/

- FileZilla - FTP and SFTP client for Mac, Linux, and Windows. https://filezilla-project.org/

- FireFTP - FTP and SFTP client Firefox that is Mac, Linux, and Windows compatible. http://fireftp.net/

- PuTTY http://www.LinuxTrainingAcademy.com/putty/

  - PSCP.EXE - SCP client for Windows

  - PSFTP.EXE - SFTP client for Windows

- Transmit - FTP and SFTP client for Mac. http://www.panic.com/transmit/

- WinSCP - FTP and SFTP client for Windows. http://winscp.net/

Customizing the Prompt

As you have seen in the "Welcome To Shell" chapter, default prompts can vary from system to system. No matter what shell you are using, you can customize your prompt by setting an environment variable. For shells like `bash`, `ksh`, and `sh` the environment variable `PS1` is used to set the primary prompt string. The shells `csh`, `tcsh`, and `zsh` use the `prompt` environment variable. The format string you place in the environment variable determines the look and feel of your prompt. Each shell uses different format strings so consult the documentation for the shell that you are using.

Let's look at customizing the bash prompt since bash is the most popular default shell for user accounts on Linux systems. These are some of the commonly used formatting string options for bash. For a complete list refer to the man page.

`\d` - the date in "Weekday Month Date" format (e.g., "Tue May 26")

`\h` - the hostname up to the first '.'

`\H` - the hostname

\n - newline

\t - the current time in 24-hour HH:MM:SS format

\T - the current time in 12-hour HH:MM:SS format

\@ - the current time in 12-hour am/pm format

\A - the current time in 24-hour HH:MM format

\u - the username of the current user

\w - the current working directory, with $HOME abbreviated with a tilde

\W - the basename of the current working directory, with $HOME abbreviated with a tilde

\$ - if the effective UID is 0, a #, otherwise a $

Here are some examples of changing the bash shell prompt by manipulating the PS1 environment variable.

```
[bob@linuxsvr ~]$ echo $PS1
[\u@\h \w]\$
[bob@linuxsvr ~]$ PS1="\u@\h \$ "
bob@linuxsvr $ PS1="<\t \u@\h \w>\$ "
<16:42:58 bob@linuxsvr ~>$ cd /tmp
<16:43:02 bob@linuxsvr /tmp>$ PS1="\d \t \h \W>\$ "
Mon Nov 18 16:45:51 linuxsvr tmp>$ PS1="\t\n[\h \w]\$ "
16:46:47
[linuxsvr /tmp]$
```

To make your customized shell prompt persist betweens logins, add the PS1 value to your personal initialization files. Personal initialization files are commonly referred to as "dot files" since they begin with a dot or period.

```
$ echo 'export PS1="[\u@\h \w]\$ "' >>
~/.bash_profile
```

Creating Aliases

If you find yourself typing the same command over and over again, you can create a shortcut for it called an alias. An alias can be thought of as a text expander. Creating aliases for commands that are really long is also a common practice. For example, if you type `ls -l` frequently, you may want to abbreviate it to `ll`. As a matter of fact, this alias often comes predefined on many Linux distributions.

`alias [name[=value]]` - List or create aliases. If no arguments are provided the current list of aliases is displayed. Use name=value to create a new alias.

```
$ ls -l
total 4
-rw-r--r-- 1 bob bob 221 Nov 13 11:30 file.txt
$ alias ll='ls -l'
$ ll
total 4
-rw-r--r-- 1 bob bob 221 Nov 13 11:30 file.txt
$ alias
alias egrep='egrep --color=auto'
alias fgrep='fgrep --color=auto'
alias grep='grep --color=auto'
alias l='ls -CF'
alias la='ls -A'
alias ll='ls -l'
alias ls='ls --color=auto'
$
```

You can even use aliases to fix common typing errors. If you find yourself typing `grpe` when you intend to type `grep`, create an alias.

```
$ alias grpe='grep'
```

Aliases can be created to make your work environment similar to that of another platform. For instance, in Windows `cls` clears the screen, but in Linux the equivalent command is `clear`. If you are coming from an

HP-UX background you are most likely familiar with the command bdf which displays disk usage. On Linux a very similar command is df. You could create these shortcuts to help you feel more at home.

```
$ alias cls='clear'
$ alias bdf='df'
```

Note that if you were to log out and log back in, your aliases would be lost. To make them persist between sessions add them to one of your personal initialization files (dot files) like .bash_profile.

The downside to creating several aliases is that when you are on a system that does not have your aliases you might feel lost. If you want to be able to work effectively on any system that you have access to, keep your alias usage to a minimum. Another way to handle this situation is to copy your configuration files to each system that you work on.

Interactive vs Non-interactive Sessions

The shell behaves in slightly different ways when you log on interactively versus when you just connect to run a single command. Here is an example to better illustrate the difference between interactive and non-interactive shells.

Interactive:

```
mac:~ bob$ ssh linuxsvr
Last login: Thu Nov  7 01:26:37 UTC 2013
Welcome to Ubuntu 12.04.3 LTS

 * Documentation:  https://help.ubuntu.com/

  System info as of Nov 14 01:26:52 UTC 2013

  System load:  0.42
  Usage of /:   3.1% of 40GB
  Memory usage: 32%
```

```
Swap usage:      0%
Processes:              89
Users logged in:       0
IP address for eth0:  10.0.0.7

bob@linuxsvr:~$ uptime
 11:49:16 up 97 days,  2:59,  5 users,  load average:
0.15,  0.25,  0.31

bob@linuxsvr:~$ ll
-rw-r--r-- 1 bob bob 221 Nov 13 11:30 file.txt
bob@linuxsvr:~$ exit
logout
Connection to 10.0.0.7 closed.
mac:~ bob$
```

Non interactive:

```
mac:~ bob$ ssh linuxsvr uptime
 11:49:16 up 97 days,  2:59,  5 users,  load average:
0.15,  0.25,  0.31
mac:~ bob$ ssh linuxsvr ll
bash: ll: command not found
mac:~ bob$
```

The contents of .profile or .bash_profile are only executed for interactive sessions. If you are not aware of this subtle difference it may leave you scratching your head as to why something works perfectly when you log in and type a command versus when you just ssh in to run that same command. For example, if you define an alias for ll in ~/.bash_profile it will work during an interactive session but it will not be available during a non-interactive session.

You can save yourself some hassle by making your interactive and non-interactive sessions behave the same. To do this, configure .bash_profile to reference .bashrc and put all of your configuration in .bashrc. You can read in the contents of another file by using the source command or dot operator.

source filename - Read and execute commands from filename and return. Any variables created or modified in filename will remain available after the script completes.

. filename - Same as source filename.

```
$ cat .bash_profile
# Put our settings in .bashrc so we have the same
environment for login and non-login shells.
if [ -f ~/.bashrc ]; then
    source ~/.bashrc
fi
$ cat .bashrc
# use a vi-style line editing interface
set -o vi

# Set the prompt.
PS1="[\u@\h \w]\$ "
export PS1

# Set the PATH.
PATH=$PATH:~/bin
export PATH

# Aliases
alias grpe='grep'
alias ll='ls -l'
alias utc='TZ=UTC date'
alias vi='vim'
```

Now the aliases you have defined are available during interactive and non-interactive sessions. Here is how the sessions behave after this change.

Interactive:

```
mac:~ bob$ ssh linuxsvr
Last login: Thu Nov  7 01:26:37 UTC 2013
Welcome to Ubuntu 12.04.3 LTS

 * Documentation:  https://help.ubuntu.com/

  System info as of Nov 14 01:26:52 UTC 2013

  System load:  0.42
  Usage of /:   3.1% of 40GB
  Memory usage: 32%
  Swap usage:    0%
  Processes:           89
  Users logged in:      0
  IP address for eth0: 10.0.0.7

bob@linuxsvr:~$ ll
-rw-r--r-- 1 bob bob 221 Nov 13 11:30 file.txt
bob@linuxsvr:~$ exit
logout
Connection to 10.0.0.7 closed.
mac:~ bob$
```

Non interactive:

```
mac:~ bob$ ssh linuxsvr ll
-rw-r--r-- 1 bob bob 221 Nov 13 11:30 file.txt
mac:~ bob$
```

Comments

In the above examples you might have noticed the octothorpe (#) followed by some very human like text in the ~/.bash_profile and ~/.bashrc files. Any text that follows an octothorpe is ignored by the shell. This is a very common pattern that not only works for shells, but also for several computer programming languages. This construct allows comments and annotations to be used without effecting the execution of a program or script.

\# - Octothorpe. Also known as a hash, square, pound sign, or number sign. This symbol precedes comments.

```
$ # This does nothing.
$ This does something.
This: command not found
$ alias # Show my aliases.
alias egrep='egrep --color=auto'
alias fgrep='fgrep --color=auto'
alias grep='grep --color=auto'
alias l='ls -CF'
alias la='ls -A'
alias ll='ls -l'
alias ls='ls --color=auto'
$
```

Shell History

The shell keeps a record of the commands you have previously executed. Bash keeps its history in memory for the current session and in the ~/.bash_history file so that it can be recalled during future sessions. Other shells may use ~/.history, ~/.zsh_history, or other similarly named files. Having access to your shell history is extremely useful because it allows you to quickly repeat commands. This can save you time, save keystrokes, prevent you from making mistakes by running a previously known good command, and generally speed up your work flow.

history - Display a list of commands in the shell history.

!N - Repeat command line number N.

!! - Repeat the previous command line.

!string - Repeat the most recent command starting with "string."

```
$ history
1 ls
2 diff secret secret.bak
3 history
$ !1
ls
PerformanceReviews tpsreports
$ echo $SHELL
/bin/bash
$ !!
echo $SHELL
/bin/bash
$ !d
diff secret secret.bak
3c3
< pass: Abee!
---
> pass: bee
$
```

With the exclamation mark history expansion syntax you can rerun a command by number. In the above example the first command in the history was executed with !1. If you want to execute the second command you would execute !2. Another convenient shortcut is !-N which means execute the Nth previous command. If you want to execute the second to last command type !-2. Since !! repeats the most recent command, it is the same as !-1.

```
$ history
1 ls
2 diff secret secret.bak
3 history
$ !-2
diff secret secret.bak
3c3
< pass: Abee!
---
> pass: bee
$
```

By default bash retains 500 commands in your shell history. This is controlled by the HISTSIZE environment variable. If you want to increase this number add export HISTSIZE=1000 or something similar to your personal initialization files.

Ctrl-r - Reverse search. Search for commands in your shell history.

You can search for commands in your history. For example, if you have the command find /var/tmp -type f in your shell history you could find it by typing Ctrl-r fi Enter. Ctrl-r initiates the reverse search and displays the search prompt, fi is the search string, and Enter executes the command that was found. You do not have to search for the start of the string. You could have very well searched for "var", "tmp", or "type."

```
$ find /var/tmp -type f
/var/tmp/file.txt
(reverse-i-search)`fi': find /var/tmp -type f
/var/tmp/file.txt
```

Tab Completion

Another way to increase your efficiency at the shell is by using tab completion. After you start typing a command you can hit the Tab key to invoke tab completion. Tab attempts to automatically complete partially typed commands. If there are multiple commands that begin with the string that precedes Tab, those commands will be displayed. You can continue to type and press Tab again. When there is only one possibility remaining, pressing the Tab key will complete the command.

Tab - Autocompletes commands and filenames.

```
$ # Typing who[Tab][Tab] results in:
$ who
who      whoami
$ # Typing whoa[Tab][Enter] results in:
$ whoami
bob
$
```

Tab completion not only works on commands, but it also works on files and directories. If you have files that start with a common prefix, Tab will expand the common component. For example, if you have two files named file1.txt and file2.txt, typing cat f Tab will expand the command line to cat file. You can then continue typing or press Tab twice to list the possible expansions. Typing cat f Tab 2 Tab will expand to cat file2.txt. After you experiment with tab completion it will soon become second nature.

```
$ # Typing cat f[Tab] results in:
$ cat file
$ # Typing: cat f[Tab][Tab][Tab] results in:
$ cat file
file1.txt   file2.txt
$ # Typing cat f[Tab] 2[Tab][Enter] results in:
$ cat file2.txt
This is file2!!!
$
```

Shell Command Line Editing

From time to time you will want to change something on your current command line. Maybe you noticed a spelling mistake at the front of the line or need to add an additional option to the current command. You may also find yourself wanting to recall a command from your shell history and modify it slightly to fit the current situation. Command line editing makes these types of activities possible.

Shells such as bash, ksh, tcsh, and zsh provide two command line editing modes. They are emacs, which is typically the default mode, and vi. Depending on the shell you can change editing modes by using the `set` or `bindkey` command. If you want to ensure your preferred mode is set upon login, add one of the two commands to your personal initialization files.

Shell	Emacs Mode	Vi Mode	Default Mode
bash	set -o emacs	set -o vi	emacs
ksh	set -o emacs	set -o vi	none
tcsh	bindkey -e	bindkey -v	emacs
zsh	bindkey -e	bindkey -v	emacs
zsh	set -o emacs	set -o vi	emacs

Emacs Mode

As you would expect, in emacs command line editing mode you can use the key bindings found in the emacs editor. For example, to move to the beginning of the command line type `Ctrl-a`. To recall the previous command type `Ctrl-p`.

`Esc Esc` - Escape completion. Similar to tab completion.

`Ctrl-b` - Move cursor to the left (back)

`Ctrl-f` - Move cursor to the right (forward)

`Ctrl-p` - Up (Previous command line)

`Ctrl-n` - Down (Next command line)

Ctrl-e - Move to the end of the line

Ctrl-a - Move to the beginning of the line

Ctrl-x Ctrl-e - Edit the current command line in the editor defined by the $EDITOR environment variable.

See the section in this book on the emacs editor for more key bindings.

Vi Mode

When you are using vi command line editing mode you start in insert mode so you can quickly type commands. To enter command mode, press Esc. To move to the previous command, for example, type Esc k. To resume editing enter insert mode by pressing i, I, a, or A.

Esc - Enter command mode.

Key bindings in command mode:

\ - Vi style file completion. Similar to tab completion.

h - Move cursor left

k - Up (Previous command line)

j - Down (Next command line)

l - Move cursor right

$ - Move to the end of the line

^ - Move to the beginning of the line

i - Enter insert mode.

a - Enter insert mode, append text at current location.

A - Enter insert mode, append text at end of line.

I - Enter insert edit mode, prepend text to start of line.

v - Edit the current command line in the editor defined by the $EDITOR environment variable.

See the section in this book on the <u>vi editor</u> for more key bindings.

Dealing with Long Shell Commands

The backslash (\) is the line continuation character. You have learned how to use the backslash to escape special characters like spaces. However, when a backslash is placed at the end of a line it is used as a line continuation character. This allows you to create command lines that are displayed as multiple lines but are executed as a single command line by the shell. You can use line continuation to make commands more readable and easier to understand.

```
$ echo "one two three"
one two three
$ echo "one \
> two \
> three"
one two three
$ echo "onetwothree"
onetwothree
$ echo "one\
> two\
> three"
onetwothree
$
```

Notice the greater-than symbol (>) in the above example. It is the secondary prompt string and can be customized by changing the PS2 environment variable. You learned previously how to change the primary prompt string with PS1 in the "Customizing the Prompt" section of this book.

```
$ PS2="line continued: "
$ echo "one \
line continued: two \
line continued: three"
one two three
$
```

Environment Variables

You have already been introduced to environment variables and have put them to good use. To recap, an environment variable is a storage location that has a name and a value. They often effect the way programs behave. For example, you learned how to inform various programs about your preferred editor by defining the $EDITOR environment variable.

Common Environment Variables

Variable	Description
EDITOR	The program to run to perform edits.
HOME	The Home directory of the user.
LOGNAME	The login name of the user.
MAIL	The location of the user's local inbox.
OLDPWD	The previous working directory.
PATH	A colon separated list of directories to search for commands.
PAGER	This program may be called to view a file.

Variable	Description
PS1	The primary prompt string.
PWD	The present working directory.
USER	The username of the user.

Viewing Environment Variables

If you know the name of the environment variable that you want to examine, you can run echo $VARIABLE_NAME or printenv VARIABLE_NAME. If you want to examine all the environment variables that are set, use the env or printenv commands.

printenv   -   Print   all   or   part   of   environment.

```
$ printenv HOME
/home/bob
$ echo $HOME
/home/bob
$ printenv
TERM=xterm-256color
SHELL=/bin/bash
USER=bob
PATH=/usr/local/bin:/usr/bin:/bin
MAIL=/var/mail/bob
PWD=/home/bob
LANG=en_US.UTF-8
HOME=/home/bob
LOGNAME=bob
$ env
TERM=xterm-256color
SHELL=/bin/bash
USER=bob
PATH=/usr/local/bin:/usr/bin:/bin
MAIL=/var/mail/bob
```

```
PWD=/home/bob
LANG=en_US.UTF-8
HOME=/home/bob
LOGNAME=bob
$
```

Exporting Environment Variables

When a process is started it inherits the exported environment variables of the process that spawned it. A variable that is set or changed only effects the current running process unless it is exported. The variables that are not exported are called local variables. The export command allows variables to be used by subsequently executed commands. Here is   an   example.

```
$ echo $PAGER

$ PAGER=less
$ echo $PAGER
less
$ bash
$ echo $PAGER

$ exit
exit
$ export PAGER=less
$ bash
$ echo $PAGER
less
$ exit
exit
$
```

In the above example PAGER was defined in the current environment. When you start a child process it inherits all the environment variables that were exported in your current environment. Since PAGER was not exported it was not set in the spawned bash shell. When you exported PAGER you saw that it was indeed available in the child process.

Removing Variables from the Environment

You can use `unset` to remove or delete an environment variable.

```
$ echo $PAGER
less
$ unset PAGER
$ echo $PAGER

$
```

Deep Dive

- Bash it - A framework for managing your bash configuration.
  https://github.com/revans/bash-it

- Command Line Completion - Tab completion explained.
  http://en.wikipedia.org/wiki/Command-line_completion

- Configuration Files for Shell - A list of files used to configure shell environments.
  http://en.wikipedia.org/wiki/Unix_shell#Configuration_files_for _shells

- Dotfiles.org - A place to upload, download, and share your dotfiles.
  http://dotfiles.org/

- Dotfiles.github.io - A guide to dotfiles on github.com.
  http://dotfiles.github.io/

- Oh my ZSH - A community-driven framework for managing your zsh configuration.
  https://github.com/robbyrussell/oh-my-zsh

- Shells

    - Bourne   Shell
      https://en.wikipedia.org/wiki/Bourne_shell

    - Bash
      https://www.gnu.org/software/bash/

    - C   Shell
      https://en.wikipedia.org/wiki/C_shell

    - Korn   Shell
      http://www.kornshell.com/

    - tcsh
      http://www.tcsh.org/

    - Z   Shell
      http://www.zsh.org/

- Using Bash History Interactively - Official Bash history
  documentation.
  http://www.gnu.org/software/bash/manual/bashref.html#Usin
  g-History-Interactively

- Unix Shell - An article on the shell user interface.
  https://en.wikipedia.org/wiki/Unix_shell

Listing Processes and Displaying Information

To display the currently running processes use the `ps` command. If no options are specified, `ps` displays the processes associated with your current session. To see every process including ones that are not owned by you, use `ps -e`. To see processes running by a specific use, use `ps -u username`.

`ps` - Display process status.

Common `ps` options:

`-e` - Everything, all processes.

`-f` - Full format listing.

`-u username` - Display processes running as username.

`-p pid` - Display process information for pid. A PID is a process ID.

Common `ps` commands:

ps -e - Display all processes.

ps -ef - Display all processes.

ps -eH - Display a process tree.

ps -e --forest - Display a process tree.

ps   -u username - Display processes running as username.

```
$ ps
  PID TTY          TIME CMD
19511 pts/2    00:00:00 bash
19554 pts/2    00:00:00 ps
$ ps -p 19511
  PID TTY          TIME CMD
19511 pts/2    00:00:00 bash
$ ps -f
UID        PID  PPID  C STIME TTY          TIME CMD
bob      19511 19509  0 16:50 pts/2    00:00:00 -bash
bob      19556 19511  0 16:50 pts/2    00:00:00 ps -f
$ ps -e | head
  PID TTY          TIME CMD
    1 ?        00:00:02 init
    2 ?        00:00:00 kthreadd
    3 ?        00:00:19 ksoftirqd/0
    5 ?        00:00:00 kworker/0:0H
    7 ?        00:00:00 migration/0
    8 ?        00:00:00 rcu_bh
    9 ?        00:00:17 rcu_sched
   10 ?        00:00:12 watchdog/0
   11 ?        00:00:00 khelper
$ ps -ef | head
UID        PID  PPID  C STIME TTY          TIME CMD
root         1     0  0 Dec27 ?        00:00:02 /sbin/init
root         2     0  0 Dec27 ?        00:00:00 [kthreadd]
root         3     2  0 Dec27 ?        00:00:19 [ksoftirqd/0]
root         5     2  0 Dec27 ?        00:00:00 [kworker/0:0H]
root         7     2  0 Dec27 ?        00:00:00 [migration/0]
root         8     2  0 Dec27 ?        00:00:00 [rcu_bh]
root         9     2  0 Dec27 ?        00:00:17 [rcu_sched]
root        10     2  0 Dec27 ?        00:00:12 [watchdog/0]
root        11     2  0 Dec27 ?        00:00:00 [khelper]
```

```
$ ps -fu www-data
UID         PID  PPID  C STIME TTY      TIME CMD
www-data    941   938  0 Dec27 ?    00:00:00
/usr/sbin/apache2 -k start
www-data    942   938  0 Dec27 ?    00:00:00
/usr/sbin/apache2 -k start
www-data    943   938  0 Dec27 ?    00:00:00
/usr/sbin/apache2 -k start
```

Here are other commands that allow you to view running processes.

pstree - Display running processes in a tree format.

htop - Interactive process viewer. This command is less common than top and may not be available on the system.

top - Interactive process viewer.

Running Processes in the Foreground and Background

Up until this point all the commands you have been executing have been running in the foreground. When a command, process, or program is running in the foreground the shell prompt will not be displayed until that process exits. For long running programs it can be convenient to send them to the background. Processes that are backgrounded still execute and perform their task, however they do not block you from entering further commands at the shell prompt. To background a process, place an ampersand (&) at the end of the command.

command & - Start command in the background.

Ctrl-c - Kill the foreground process.

Ctrl-z - Suspend the foreground process.

bg [%num] - Background a suspended process.

fg [%num] - Foreground a background process.

kill [%num] - Kill a process by job number or PID.

jobs [%num] - List jobs.

```
$ ./long-running-program &
[1] 22686
$ ps -p 22686
  PID TTY              TIME CMD
22686 pts/1        00:00:00 long-running-pr
$ jobs
[1]+  Running   ./long-running-program &
$ fg
./long-running-program
```

When a command is backgrounded two numbers are displayed. The number in brackets is the job number and can be referred by preceding it with the percent sign. The second number is the PID. Here is what it looks like to start multiple processes in the background.

```
$ ./long-running-program &
[1] 22703
$ ./long-running-program &
[2] 22705
$ ./long-running-program &
[3] 22707
$ ./long-running-program &
[4] 22709


$ jobs
[1]   Done        ./long-running-program
[2]   Done        ./long-running-program
[3]-  Running     ./long-running-program &
[4]+  Running     ./long-running-program &
```

The plus sign (+) in the jobs output represents the current job while the minus sign (-) represents the previous job. The current job is considered to be the last job that was stopped while it was in the foreground or the last job started in the background. The current job can be referred to by %% or %+. If no job information is supplied to the fg or bg commands, the current job is operated upon. The previous job can be referred to by %-.

You will notice that jobs number 1 and 2 are reported as being done. The shell does not interrupt your current command line, but will report job statuses right before a new prompt is displayed. For example, if you start a program in the background a prompt is returned. The shell will not report the status of the job until a new prompt is displayed. You can request a new prompt be displayed by simply hitting Enter.

To bring a job back to the foreground, type the name of the job or use the fg command. To foreground the current job execute %%, %+, fg, fg %%, fg %+, or fg %num. To foreground job number 3, execute %3 or fg %3.

```
$ jobs
[3]-  Running          ./long-running-program &
[4]+  Running          ./long-running-program &
$ fg %3
./long-running-program
```

To pause or suspend a job that is running in the foreground, type Ctrl-z. Once a job is suspended it can be resumed in the foreground or background. To background a suspended job type the name of the job followed by an ampersand or use bg followed by the job name.

```
$ jobs
[1]   Running    ./long-running-program &
[2]-  Running    ./long-running-program &
[3]+  Running    ./another-program &
$ fg
./another-program
^Z
[3]+  Stopped    ./another-program
```

```
$ jobs
[1]    Running     ./long-running-program &
[2]-   Running     ./long-running-program &
[3]+   Stopped     ./another-program
$ bg %3
[3]+ ./another-program &
$ jobs
[1]    Running     ./long-running-program &
[2]-   Running     ./long-running-program &
[3]+   Running     ./another-program &
```

You can stop or kill a background job using the `kill` command. For example, to kill job number 1 execute `kill %1`. To kill a job that is running in the foreground, type `Ctrl-c`.

```
$ jobs
[1]    Running       ./long-running-program &
[2]-   Running       ./long-running-program &
[3]+   Running       ./another-program &
$ kill %1
[1]    Terminated    ./long-running-program
$ jobs
[2]-   Running       ./long-running-program &
[3]+   Running       ./another-program &
$ fg %2
./long-running-program
^C
$ jobs
[3]+   Running       ./another-program &
$
```

Killing Processes

`Ctrl-c` - Kills the foreground process.

`kill [signal] pid` - Send a signal to a process.

`kill -l` - Display a list of signals.

The default signal used by kill is termination. You will see this signal referred to as SIGTERM or TERM for short. Signals have numbers that correspond to their names. The default TERM signal is number 15. So running kill pid, kill -15 pid, and kill -TERM pid are all equivalent. If a process does not terminate when you send it the TERM signal, use the KILL signal which is number 9.

```
$ ps | grep hard-to-stop
27398 pts/1    00:00:00 hard-to-stop
$ kill 27398
$ ps | grep hard-to-stop
27398 pts/1    00:00:00 hard-to-stop
$ kill -9 27398
$ ps | grep hard-to-stop
$
```

Deep Dive

- Bash Documentation on Job Control
  http://gnu.org/software/bash/manual/html_node/Job-Control.html

SCHEDULING REPEATED JOBS WITH CRON

If you need to repeat a task on a schedule, you can use the cron service. Every minute the cron service checks to see if there are any scheduled jobs to run and if so runs them. Cron jobs are often used to automate a process or perform routine maintenance. You can schedule cron jobs by using the `crontab` command.

`cron` - A time based job scheduling service. This service is typically started when the system boots.

`crontab` - A program to create, read, update, and delete your job schedules.

A crontab (cron table) is a configuration file that specifies when commands are to be executed by cron. Each line in a crontab represents a job and contains two pieces of information: 1) when to run and 2) what to run. The time specification consists of five fields. They are minutes, hour, day of the month, month, and day of the week. After the time specification you provide the command to be executed.

Crontab Format

```
* * * * * command
| | | | |
| | | | +-- Day of the Week    (0-6)
| | | +---- Month of the Year  (1-12)
| | +------ Day of the Month   (1-31)
| +-------- Hour               (0-23)
+---------- Minute             (0-59)
```

The command will only be executed when all of the time specification fields match the current date and time. You can specify that a command be run only once, but this is not the typical use case for cron. Typically, one or more of the time specification fields will contain an asterisk (*) which matches any time or date for that field. Here is an example crontab.

```
# Run every Monday at 07:00.
0 7 * * 1 /opt/sales/bin/weekly-report
```

Here is a graphical representation of the above crontab entry.

```
0 7 * * 1 /opt/sales/bin/weekly-report
| | | | |
| | | | +-- Day of the Week    (0-6)
| | | +---- Month of the Year  (1-12)
| | +------ Day of the Month   (1-31)
| +-------- Hour               (0-23)
+---------- Minute             (0-59)
```

This job will run only when the minute is 0, the hour is 7, and the day of the week is 1. In the day of the week field 0 represents Sunday, 1 Monday, etc. This job will run on any day and during any month since the asterisk was used for those two fields.

If any output is generated by the command it is mailed to you. You can check your local mail with the mail command. If you would prefer not to get email you can redirect the output of the command as in this example.

```
# Run at 02:00 every day and send output to a log.
0 2 * * * /opt/acme/bin/backup > /tmp/backup.log 2>&1
```

You can provide multiple values for each of the fields. If you would like to run a command every half-hour, you could do this.

```
# Run every 30 minutes.
0,30 * * * * /opt/acme/bin/half-hour-check
```

```
# Another way to do the same thing.
*/2 * * * * /opt/acme/bin/half-hour-check
```

Instead of using 0,30 for the minute field you could have used */2. You can even use ranges with a dash. If you want to run a job every minute for the first four minutes of the hour you can use this time specification: 0-4 * * * * command.

There are several implementations of the cron scheduler and some allow you to use shortcuts and keywords in your crontabs. Common keywords have been provided below, but refer to the documentation for cron on your system to ensure these will work.

Keyword	Description	Equivalent
@yearly	Run once a year at midnight in the morning of January 1	0 0 1 1 *
@annually	Same as @yearly	0 0 1 1 *
@monthly	Run once a month at midnight in the morning of the first day of the month	0 0 1 * *
@weekly	Run once a week at midnight in the morning of Sunday	0 0 * * 0
@daily	Run once a day at midnight	0 0 * * *
@midnight	Same as @daily	0 0 * * *
@hourly	Run once an hour at the beginning of the hour	0 * * * *
@reboot	Run at startup	N/A

Using the Crontab Command

Use the `crontab` command to manipulate cron jobs.

`crontab file` - Install a new crontab from file.

`crontab -l` - List your cron jobs.

`crontab -e` - Edit your cron jobs.

`crontab -r` - Remove all of your cron jobs.

```
$ crontab -l
no crontab for bob
$ cat my-cron
# Run every Monday at 07:00.
0 7 * * 1 /opt/sales/bin/weekly-report
$ crontab my-cron
$ crontab -l
# Run every Monday at 07:00.
0 7 * * 1 /opt/sales/bin/weekly-report
$ crontab -e
# $EDITOR is invoked.
$ crontab -r
$ crontab -l
no crontab for bob
$
```

Deep Dive

- CronWFT - Decodes crontab lines. Print out human readable output.
  http://cronwtf.github.io/

- CronMaker - A utility which helps you to build cron expressions.
  http://www.cronmaker.com/

SWITCHING USERS AND RUNNING COMMANDS AS OTHERS

su

One way to start a session as another user on the system is to use the su command. If no arguments are supplied to su, it assumes you are trying to become the superuser. Executing su is the same as executing su root. Your current environment is passed to the new shell unless you specify a hyphen (-). In that case, su creates an environment like you would expect to see had you logged in as that user.

su [username] - Change user ID or become superuser

Common su options:

- - A hyphen is used to provide an environment similar to what the user would expect had the user logged in directly.

-c command - Specify a command to be executed. If the command is more than one word in length, it needs to be quoted.

```
bob@linuxsvr:~$ export TEST=1
bob@linuxsvr:~$ su oracle
Password:
oracle@linuxsvr:/home/bob$ echo $TEST
1
oracle@linuxsvr:/home/bob$ pwd
/home/bob
oracle@linuxsvr:/home/bob$ exit
exit
bob@linuxsvr:~$ su - oracle
Password:
oracle@linuxsvr:~$ echo $TEST

oracle@linuxsvr:~$ pwd
/home/oracle
oracle@linuxsvr:~$ exit
bob@linuxsvr:~$ su -c 'echo $ORACLE_HOME' oracle
Password:

bob@linuxsvr:~$ su -c 'echo $ORACLE_HOME' - oracle
Password:
/u01/app/oracle/product/current
bob@linuxsvr:~$
```

If you want to know what user you are working as, run the whoami command.

whoami - Displays the effective username.

```
$ whoami
bob
$ su oracle
Password:
$ whoami
oracle
$
```

Sudo - Super User Do

Another way to switch users or execute commands as others is to use the `sudo` command. Sudo allows you to run programs with the security privileges of another user. Like `su`, if no username is specified it assumes you are trying to run commands as the superuser. This is why sudo is referred to as super user do. It is commonly used to install, start, and stop applications that require superuser privileges.

`sudo` - Execute a command as another user, typically the superuser.

One advantage of using `sudo` over the `su` command is that you do not need to know the password of the other user. This can eliminate the issues that arise from using shared passwords and generic accounts. When you execute the `sudo` command you are prompted for your password. If the sudo configuration permits access, the command is executed. The sudo configuration is typically controlled by the system administrator and requires root access to change.

Using Sudo

Here are the common ways to use the `sudo` command.

`sudo -1` - List available commands.

`sudo command` - Run command as the superuser.

`sudo -u root command` - Same as **sudo** command.

`sudo -u user command` - Run command as user.

`sudo su` - Switch to the superuser account.

`sudo su -` - Switch to the superuser account with an environment like you would expect to see had you logged in as that user.

`sudo su - username` - Switch to the username account with an environment like you would expect to see had you logged in as that user.

```
$ sudo -l
User bob may run the following commands on this host:
(root) NOPASSWD: /etc/init.d/apache2
(fred) NOPASSWD: /opt/fredApp/bin/start
(fred) NOPASSWD: /opt/fredApp/bin/stop
(root) /bin/su - oracle
$ sudo /etc/init.d/apache2 start
 * Starting web server apache2
$ sudo -u fred /opt/fredApp/bin/start
Fred's app started as user fred.
$ sudo su - oracle
[sudo] password for bob:
oracle@linuxsvr:~$ whoami
oracle
oracle@linuxsvr:~$ exit
$ whoami
bob
$
```

The output of sudo -l displays what commands can be executed with sudo and under which account. In the above example, sudo will not prompt for a password for the commands preceded with NOPASSWD. This type of configuration may be required to automate jobs via cron that require escalated privileges.

Deep Dive

- The su command
  http://www.linfo.org/su.html

- Sudo - The official sudo website.
  http://www.sudo.ws/sudo/

- Ubuntu Sudo Documentation
  http://help.ubuntu.com/community/RootSudo

INSTALLING SOFTWARE

Typically when you install software on a Linux system you do so with a package. A package is a collection of files that make up an application. Additionally, a package contains data about the application as well as any steps required to successfully install and remove that application. The data, or metadata, that is contained within a package can include information such as the description of the application, the version of the application, and a list of other packages that it depends on. In order to install or remove a package you need to use superuser privileges.

A package manager is used to install, upgrade, and remove packages. Any additional software that is required for a package to function properly is known as a dependency. The package manager uses a package's metadata to automatically install the dependencies. Package managers keep track of what files belong to what packages, what packages are installed, and what versions of those packages are installed.

Installing Software on CentOS, Fedora, and RedHat Distributions

The `yum` command line utility is a package management program for

Linux distributions that use the RPM package manager. CentOS, Fedora, Oracle Linux, RedHat Enterprise Linux, and Scientific Linux are RPM based distributions on which you can use yum.

yum search search-string - Search for search-string.

yum install [-y] package - Install package. Use the -y option to automatically answer yes to yum's questions.

yum remove package - Remove/uninstall package.

yum info [package] - Display information about package.

To search for software to install, use yum search search-string.

```
$ yum search inkscape
Loaded plugins: refresh-packagekit, security
============= N/S Matched: inkscape =============
inkscape-docs.i686 : Documentation for Inkscape
inkscape.i686 : Vector-based drawing program using
SVG
inkscape-view.i686 : Viewing program for SVG files

  Name and summary matches only, use "search all" for
everything.
$
```

To install software, use yum install package. Installing software requires superuser privileges. This means you need to use sudo or switch to the root account with the su command.

```
$ sudo yum install inkscape
[sudo] password for bob:
Loaded plugins: refresh-packagekit, security
Setting up Install Process
Resolving Dependencies
--> Running transaction check
---> Package inkscape.i686 0:0.47-6.el6 will be
installed
```

JASON CANNON

```
--> Processing Dependency: python for package:
...
Dependencies Resolved
=======================================================
 Package     Arch   Version            Repository
Size
=======================================================
Installing:
 inkscape    i686  0.47-6.el6          base        8.6 M
Installing for dependencies:
 ImageMagick i686  6.5.4.7-7.el6_5  updates       1.7 M
...
Transaction Summary
=======================================================
Install     21 Package(s)

Total download size: 21 M
Installed size: 97 M
Is this ok [y/N]: y
Downloading Packages:
(1/21): ImageMagick-6.5.4.7-7.el6_5.i686.rpm
...
Installed:
  inkscape.i686 0:0.47-6.el6

Dependency Installed:
  ImageMagick.i686 0:6.5.4.7-7.el6_5
...
Complete!
```

To uninstall a package, use yum remove. Removing software requires superuser privileges.

```
$ sudo yum remove inkscape
Loaded plugins: refresh-packagekit, security
Setting up Remove Process
Resolving Dependencies
--> Running transaction check
---> Package inkscape.i686 0:0.47-6.el6 will be
erased
--> Finished Dependency Resolution
```

```
Dependencies Resolved

===========================================================
 Package    Arch    Version       Repository       Size
===========================================================
Removing:
 inkscape   i686    0.47-6.el6    @base            37 M

Transaction Summary
===========================================================
Remove         1 Package(s)

Installed size: 37 M
Is this ok [y/N]: y
Downloading Packages:
Running rpm_check_debug
Running Transaction Test
Transaction Test Succeeded
Running Transaction
  Erasing    : inkscape-0.47-6.el6.i686     1/1
  Verifying  : inkscape-0.47-6.el6.i686     1/1

Removed:
  inkscape.i686 0:0.47-6.el6

Complete!
$
```

The rpm Command

In addition to the yum command, you can use the rpm command to interact with the package manager.

rpm -qa - List all the installed packages.

rpm -qf /path/to/file - List the package that contains file.

rpm -ivh package.rpm - Install a package from the file named

173

package.rpm.

`rpm -ql package` - List all files that belong to package

```
$ rpm -qa | sort | head
acl-2.2.49-6.el6.i686
acpid-1.0.10-2.1.el6.i686
aic94xx-firmware-30-2.el6.noarch
alsa-lib-1.0.22-3.el6.i686
alsa-plugins-pulseaudio-1.0.21-3.el6.i686
alsa-utils-1.0.22-5.el6.i686
anaconda-13.21.215-1.el6.centos.i686
anaconda-yum-plugins-1.0-5.1.el6.noarch
apache-tomcat-apis-0.1-1.el6.noarch
apr-1.3.9-5.el6_2.i686
$ rpm -qf /usr/bin/which
which-2.19-6.el6.i686
$ sudo rpm -ivh SpiderOak-5.0.3-1.i386.rpm
[sudo] password for bob:
Preparing...        ####################### [100%]
   1:SpiderOak       ####################### [100%]
$
```

Installing Software on Debian and Ubuntu

The Debian and Ubuntu distributions use a package manager called APT, the Advanced Packaging Tool. APT is comprised of a few small utilities with the two most commonly used ones being `apt-cache` and `apt-get`.

`apt-cache search search-string` - Search for search-string.

`apt-get install [-y] package` - Install package. Use the `-y` option to automatically answer yes to apt-get's questions.

`apt-get remove package` - Remove/uninstall package, leaving behind configuration files.

`apt-get purge package` - Remove/uninstall package, deleting configuration files.

apt-cache show package - Display information about package.

To search for software to install, use apt-cache search search-string.

```
$ apt-cache search inkscape
create-resources - shared resources for use by
creative applications
inkscape - vector-based drawing program
python-scour - SVG scrubber and optimizer
fonts-opendin - Open DIN font
fonts-rufscript - handwriting-based font for Latin
characters
ink-generator - Inkscape extension to automatically
generate files from a template
lyx - document processor
robocut - Control program for Graphtec cutting
plotters
sozi - inkscape extension for creating animated
presentations
ttf-rufscript - handwriting-based font for Latin
characters (transitional dummy package)
$
```

To install software, use apt-get install package. Installing software requires superuser privileges. This means you need to use sudo or switch to the root account with the su command.

```
$ sudo apt-get install inkscape
Reading package lists... Done
Building dependency tree
Reading state information... Done
The following extra packages will be installed:
  aspell aspell-en cmap-adobe-japan1 dbus-x11
...
3 upgraded, 74 newly installed, 0 to remove and 96
not upgraded.
Need to get 62.7 MB of archives.
After this operation, 171 MB of additional disk space
```

```
will be used.
Do you want to continue [Y/n]? y
...
Setting up perlmagick (8:6.6.9.7-5ubuntu3.2) ...
Processing triggers for libc-bin ...
ldconfig deferred processing now taking place
$
```

To uninstall a package, use apt-get remove. Removing software requires superuser privileges.

```
$ sudo apt-get remove inkscape
Reading package lists... Done
Building dependency tree
Reading state information... Done
The following packages will be REMOVED:
  inkscape
0 upgraded, 0 newly installed, 1 to remove and 96 not
upgraded.
After this operation, 64.9 MB disk space will be
freed.
Do you want to continue [Y/n]? y
(Reading database ... 69841 files and directories
currently installed.)
Removing inkscape ...
Processing triggers for man-db ...
Processing triggers for hicolor-icon-theme ...
$
```

The dpkg Command

In addition the apt utilities, you can use the dpkg command to interact with the package manager.

dgpk -l - List all the installed packages.

dpkg -S /path/to/file - List the package that contains file.

dpkg -i package.rpm - Install a package from the file named package.deb.

`dpkg -L package` - List all files that belong to package.

```
$ dpkg -l | head
Desired=Unknown/Install/Remove/Purge/Hold
| Status=Not/Inst/Conf-files/Unpacked/halF-conf/Half-
inst/trig-aWait/Trig-pend
|/ Err?=(none)/Reinst-required (Status,Err:
uppercase=bad)
||/ Name              Version
Description
+++-==================-=============-==================
ii  accountsservice   0.6.15-2ubuntu9.6      query
and manipulate user account information
ii  acpid             1:2.0.10-1ubuntu3      Advanced
Configuration and Power Interface event daemon
ii  adduser           3.113ubuntu2           add and
remove users and groups
ii  apparmor          2.7.102-0ubuntu3.9     User-
space parser utility for AppArmor
ii  apport            2.0.1-0ubuntu17.5
automatically generate crash reports for debugging
$ dpkg -S /usr/bin/which
debianutils: /usr/bin/which
$ sudo dpkg -i spideroak_5.1.3_i386.deb
[sudo] password for bob:
Selecting previously unselected package spideroak.
(Reading database ... 153942 files and directories
currently installed.)
Unpacking spideroak (from spideroak_5.1.3_i386.deb)
...
Setting up spideroak (1:5.1.3) ...
Processing triggers for man-db ...
Processing triggers for desktop-file-utils ...
Processing triggers for bamfdaemon ...
Rebuilding /usr/share/applications/bamf.index...
Processing triggers for gnome-menus ...
$
```

Deep Dive

- Managing Software with Yum
  https://www.centos.org/docs/5/html/yum/

- AptGet Howto
  https://help.ubuntu.com/community/AptGet/Howto

- Ubuntu - Installing Software
  https://help.ubuntu.com/community/InstallingSoftware

THE END AND THE BEGINNING

Even though this is the end of this book, I sincerely hope that it is just the beginning of your Linux journey. Linux has been growing steadily in popularity since its release in 1991. You will find Linux running on phones, laptops, servers, supercomputers, industrial equipment, and even on medical devices. The possibilities for learning, exploring, and growing are endless.

ABOUT THE AUTHOR

Jason Cannon started his career as a Unix and Linux System Engineer in 1999. Since that time he has utilized his Linux skills at companies such as Xerox, UPS, Hewlett-Packard, and Amazon.com. Additionally, he has acted as a technical consultant and independent contractor for small to medium businesses.

Jason has professional experience with CentOS, RedHat Enterprise Linux, SUSE Linux Enterprise Server, and Ubuntu. He has used several Linux distributions on personal projects including Debian, Slackware, CrunchBang, and others. In addition to Linux, Jason has experience supporting proprietary Unix operating systems including AIX, HP-UX, and Solaris.

He enjoys teaching others how to use and exploit the power of the Linux operating system and teaches online video training courses at http://www.LinuxTrainingAcademy.com.

Jason is also the author of *The Linux Screenshot Tour Book: An Illustrated Guide to the Most Popular Linux Distributions* and *Command Line Kung Fu: Bash Scripting Tricks, Linux Shell ProgrammingTips, and Bash One-Liners.*

APPENDICES

APPENDIX A:
ABBREVIATIONS AND ACRONYMS

ACL - access control list

APT - advanced packaging tool (apt)

ASCII - American Standard Code for Information Interchange

CentOS - Community ENTerprise Operating System

cd - Change directory

CLI - command line interface

crontab - cron table

dir - directory

distro - Distribution, a collection of user programs, software, and the Linux kernel to create an operating environment.

FOSS - free open source software

FTP - file transfer protocol

GID - group identification

GB - gigabyte

GNU - GNU's Not UNIX. (See GNU.org)

GUI - graphical user interface

HP - Hewlett-Packard

IBM - International Business Machines

KB - kilobyte

I/O - input/output

LFS - Linux from scratch.
(See http://www.linuxfromscratch.org/)

LSB - Linux Standard Base

LUG - Linux user group

LVM - logical volume management

MB - megabyte

MBR - master boot record

NFS - network file system

NTP - network time protocol

OS - operating system

PID - process identification number

POSIX - portable operating system interface

pwd - present working directory

RHEL - RedHat Enterprise Linux

RHCE - Red Hat Certified Engineer

RPM - RedHat Package Manager

SAN - storage area network

SELinux - Security Enhanced Linux

SFTP - secure file transfer protocol or SSH file transfer protocol

SGID - set group ID

SLES - SuSE Linux Enterprise Server

SSH - secure shell

STDIN - Standard input

STDOUT - Standard output

STDERR - Standard error

su - superuser

sudo - superuser do

SUID - set user ID

symlink - symbolic link

tar - tape archive

TB - terabyte

TTY - teletype terminal

UID - user identification

VDI - virtual disk image

X - X window system

YUM - Yellowdog Updater, Modified (yum)

APPENDIX B: FAQ

Q: Where can I access all the links in this book?

The links covered in this book along with other supplemental material is available at:

http://www.linuxtrainingacademy.com/lfb

Q: What is Linux?

Linux is an open-source operating system modelled after UNIX.

Q: What is the Linux kernel?

The Linux kernel handles the interactions between the software running on the system and the hardware. To learn more, visit the official Linux kernel website at http://www.kernel.org.

Q: Which Linux distribution should I use?

If your goal is to eventually become a Linux system administrator, focus on CentOS or Ubuntu. CentOS is a Red Hat Enterprise Linux (RHEL) derivative. As a general rule, CentOS and RHEL are often found in corporate environments. Ubuntu is popular with startups and smaller companies that run their operations in the cloud. If you are using Linux for your own personal reasons, choose a distribution that appeals to you. To get some ideas look at DistroWatch.com's top 10 distributions page.

Here are some other common Linux distributions:

- Arch Linux - https://www.archlinux.org/

- Debian - http://www.debian.org/

- Fedora - http://fedoraproject.org/

- LinuxMint - http://www.linuxmint.com/

- Mageia - http://www.mageia.org/

- openSUSE - http://www.opensuse.org/

There are several special purpose Linux distributions that focus on a single area. Examples areas of focus include education, minimalism, multimedia, networking/firewalls, and security. Here is just a sampling of the available specialty distros.

- ArtistX - A DVD which turns a computer into a full multimedia production studio.
  http://artistx.org/

- Edubuntu - An education oriented operating system.
  http://www.edubuntu.com/

- live.linuX-gamers.net - A live Linux distribution focused on gaming.
  http://live.linux-gamers.net/

- Mythbuntu - Mythbuntu is focused upon setting up a standalone MythTV based PVR (personal video recorder)

system.
http://www.mythbuntu.org/

- Parted Magic - A Hard disk management solution.
https://partedmagic.com/

- Scientific Linux - Scientific Linux is put together by Fermilab, CERN, and various other labs and universities around the world. Its primary purpose is to reduce duplicated effort of the labs, and to have a common install base for the various experimenters.
https://www.scientificlinux.org/

- Ubuntu Studio - Provides the full range of multimedia content creation applications for audio, graphics, video, photography and publishing.
http://ubuntustudio.org/

- VortexBox - VortexBox is a multifunctional solution to rip, store and stream CDs, digital music and Internet radio.
http://www.vortexbox.co.uk/

Q: Can I use Microsoft Office in Linux?

Microsoft Office is not available for Linux, however there are alternatives such as Libreoffice, Open Office, and AbiWord.

Q: How do I run XYZ program in Linux?

To find Linux alternatives for software you use on Mac and Windows, visit http://alternativeto.net/.

APPENDIX C: TRADEMARKS

BSD/OS is a trademark of Berkeley Software Design, Inc. in the United States and other countries.

Facebook is a registered trademark of Facebook, Inc..

Firefox is a registered trademark of the Mozilla Foundation.

HP and HEWLETT-PACKARD are registered trademarks that belong to Hewlett-Packard Development Company, L.P.

IBM® is a registered trademark of International Business Machines Corp., registered in many jurisdictions worldwide.

Linux® is the registered trademark of Linus Torvalds in the U.S. and other countries.

Mac and OS X are trademarks of Apple Inc., registered in the U.S. and other countries.

Open Source is a registered certification mark of Open Source Initiative.

Sun and Oracle Solaris are trademarks or registered trademarks of Oracle Corporatoin and/or its affiliates in the United States and other countries.

UNIX is a registered trademark of The Open Group.

Windows is a registered trademark of Microsoft Corporation in the United States and other countries.

All other product names mentioned herein are the trademarks of their respective owners.

Command Line
Kung Fu

JASON CANNON

JASON CANNON

CONTENTS

INTRODUCTION

I have been working at the command line on Unix and Linux systems since the 1990's. Needless to say, I feel right at home with nothing more than a dollar sign and a flashing cursor staring at me. Over the years I've picked up several command line "tricks" that have saved me time and frustration.

Some of these tips were born out of necessity — I simply had too much work to complete and too little time to do it in. Others were modeled after popular patterns found in computer programming and application development. The rest were shared with me, either directly or indirectly, by my command line heroes and mentors. It's amazing what you can learn by watching, emulating, and taking advice from a seasoned Unix and Linux professional.

Even though the title is *Command Line Kung Fu*, you don't have to be a Linux ninja to use the tactics presented in this book. The tips work as presented. You can start putting them to use immediately without fully understanding all the details and nuances. However, if you want or need more information, explanations and practical real-world examples follow each one.

Also, if you want an overview of the Linux command line and operating system please read my other book *Linux for Beginners*. It will give you a strong foundation upon which you can build your Linux skills.

Let's get started.

SHELL HISTORY

Run the Last Command as Root

```
$ sudo !!
$ su -c "!!"
```

If you ever forget to run a command with root privileges, you can simply repeat it by using sudo !! or su -c "!!".

```
$ adduser sam
-bash: /usr/sbin/adduser: Permission denied
$ sudo !!
sudo adduser sam
$ id sam
uid=1007(sam) gid=1007(sam) groups=1007(sam)
$ userdel -r sam
-bash: /usr/sbin/userdel: Permission denied
$ sudo !!
```

```
sudo userdel -r sam
$ id sam
id: sam: No such user
$ useradd jim
-bash: /usr/sbin/useradd: Permission denied
$ su -c "!!"
su -c "useradd jim"
Password:
$ id jim
uid=1007(jim) gid=1007(jim) groups=1007(jim)
```

This exclamation mark syntax is called an event designator. An event designator references a command in your shell history. Bang-Bang (!!) repeats the most recent command, but one of my favorite uses of the event designator is to run the most recent command that starts with a given string. Here's an example.

```
$ whoami
jason
$ uptime
12:33:15 up 35 min, 1 user, load average: 0.00, 0.00,
0.00
$ df -hT /boot
Filesystem Type Size Used Avail Use% Mounted on
/dev/vda1 ext4 485M 55M 406M 12% /boot
$ !u
uptime
12:33:29 up 35 min, 1 user, load average: 0.00, 0.00,
0.00
```

```
$ sudo !w
sudo whoami
root
```

Repeat the Last Command That Started with a given String

```
$ !<string>
```

This is another example of an event designator. To recall the most recent command that begins with <string>, run "!<string>". You can simply specify the first letter, or as much of the string to make it unique. This example demonstrates that concept.

```
$ who
jason          pts/1  2014-04-06 21:04 (192.168.1.117)
$ w
jason          pts/1        192.168.1.117 21:04 0.00s
0.33s 0.00s w
$ !w
w
jason          pts/1        192.168.1.117 21:04 0.00s
0.33s 0.00s w
$ !wh
who
jason          pts/1  2014-04-06 21:04 (192.168.1.117)
```

Here is a practical example where you check to see if a process is running, kill it, and confirm that it did indeed stop.

```
$ ps -fu apache
```

```
UID     PID  PPID  C STIME TTY  TIME CMD
apache 1877 1879  0 21:32 ?    00:00:00
/usr/sbin/httpd
apache 1879 1     0 21:32 ?    00:00:00
/usr/sbin/httpd
$ sudo service httpd stop
Stopping httpd:          [  OK  ]
$ !p
ps -fu apache
UID     PID  PPID  C STIME TTY  TIME CMD
$
```

Reuse the Second Word (First Argument) from the Previous Command

```
$ !^
```

If you need to grab the second word from the previous command, you can use the "!^" word designator. Wherever you use "!^" it will be replaced by the second word from the previous command. You can also think of this as the first argument to the previous command.

```
$ host www.google.com 8.8.8.8
Using domain server:
Name: 8.8.8.8
Address: 8.8.8.8#53
Aliases:
www.google.com has address 173.194.46.83
www.google.com has address 173.194.46.81
www.google.com has address 173.194.46.84
www.google.com has address 173.194.46.82
```

www.google.com has address 173.194.46.80

www.google.com has IPv6 address
2607:f8b0:4009:805::1013

$ ping -c1 !^

ping -c1 www.google.com

PING www.google.com (173.194.46.80) 56(84) bytes of data.

64 bytes from ord08s11-in-f16.1e100.net (173.194.46.80): icmp_seq=1 ttl=51 time=17.0 ms

--- www.google.com ping statistics ---

1 packets transmitted, 1 received, 0% packet loss, time 49ms

rtt min/avg/max/mdev = 17.071/17.071/17.071/0.000 ms

$

Reuse the Last Word (Last Argument) from the Previous Command

$!$

Quite often I find myself needing to perform another operation on the last item on the previous command line. To access that item in your current command, use "!$".

$ unzip tpsreport.zip

Archive: tpsreport.zip

  inflating: cover-sheet.doc

$ rm !$

rm tpsreport.zip

$ mv cover-sheet.doc reports/

$ du -sh !$

```
du -sh reports/
4.7G  reports/
$
```

Reuse the Nth Word from a Previous Command

```
$ !!:N
$ <event_designator>:<number>
```

To access a word in the previous command use "!!:N" where N is the number of the word you wish to retrieve. The first word is 0, the second word is 1, etc. You can think of 0 as being the command, 1 as being the first argument to the command, 2 as being the second argument, and so on.

You can use any event designator in conjunction with a word designator. In the following example, "!!" is the most recent command line: avconv -i screencast.mp4 podcast.mp3. The "!a" event designator expands to that same command since it's the most recent command that started with the letter "a."

```
$ avconv -i screencast.mp4 podcast.mp3
$ mv !!:2 converted/
mv screencast.mp4 converted/
$ mv !a:3 podcasts/
mv podcast.mp3 podcasts/
$
```

Repeat the Previous Command While Substituting a String

```
$ ^<string1>^<string2>^
```

This little trick is great for quickly correcting typing mistakes. If you omit ^<string2>^, then <string1> will be removed from the previous command. By default, only the first occurrence of <string1> is replaced. To replace every occurrence, append ":&". You can omit the trailing caret symbol, except when using ":&".

```
$ grpe jason /etc/passwd
-bash: grpe: command not found
$ ^pe^ep
grep jason /etc/passwd
jason:x:501:501:Jason Cannon:/home/jason:/bin/bash
$ grep rooty /etc/passwd
$ ^y
grep root /etc/passwd
root:x:0:0:root:/root:/bin/bash
operator:x:11:0:operator:/root:/sbin/nologin
$ grep canon /etc/passwd ; ls -ld /home/canon
ls: cannot access /home/canon: No such file or
directory
$ ^canon^cannon^:&
grep cannon /etc/passwd ; ls -ld /home/cannon
cannon:x:1001:1001::/home/cannon:/bin/sh
drwxr-xr-x 2 cannon ball 4096 Apr  7 00:22 /home/cannon
```

Reference a Word of the Current Command and Reuse It

```
$ !#:N
```

The "!#" event designator represents the current command line, while the :N word designator represents a word on the command line. Word references are zero based, so the first word, which is almost always a command, is :0, the second word, or first argument to the command, is :1, etc.

```
$ mv Working-with-Files.pdf Chapter-18-!#:1
mv Working-with-Files.pdf Chapter-18-Working-with-
Files.pdf
```

Save a Copy of Your Command Line Session

```
$ script
```

If you want to document what you see on your screen, use the script command. The script command captures everything that is printed on your terminal and saves it to a file. You can provide script a file name as an argument or let it create the default file named typescript.

```
$ script
Script started, file is typescript
$ cd /usr/local/bin
$ sudo ./upgradedb.sh
sudo password for jason:
Starting database upgrade.
...
Database upgrade complete.
$ exit
exit
Script done, file is typescript
$ cat typescript
Script started on Wed 09 Apr 2014 06:30:58 PM EDT
$ cd /usr/local/bin
$ sudo ./upgradedb.sh
sudo password for jason:
```

```
Starting database upgrade.

...

Database upgrade complete.

$ exit

exit

Script done on Wed 09 Apr 2014 06:31:44 PM EDT

$
```

Find out Which Commands You Use Most Often

```
$ history | awk '{print $2}' | sort | uniq -c | sort
-rn | head
```

To get a list of the top ten most used commands in your shell history, use the following command.

```
$ history | awk '{print $2}' | sort | uniq -c | sort
-rn | head
          61 ls
          45 cd
          40 cat
          31 vi
          24 ip
          22 sudo
          22 ssh
          22 ll
          19 rm
          17 find
$
```

Clear Your Shell History

```
$ history -c
```

To clear your shell history, use the -c option to the history command.

```
$ history | tail -5
  966  ls -lR Music/
  967  find Music/ -type f -ls
  968  dstat
  969  sudo vi /etc/motd
  970  cd ..
  971  sudo du -s /home/* | sort -n
$ history -c
$ history
    1  history
$
```

TEXT PROCESSING AND MANIPULATION

Strip out Comments and Blank Lines

```
$ grep -E -v "^#|^$" file
```

To strip out all the noise from a configuration file get rid of the comments and blank lines. These two regexes (regular expressions) do the trick. "^#" matches all lines that begin with a "#". "^$" matches all blank lines. The -E option to grep allows us to use regexes and the -v option inverts the matches.

```
[jason@www conf]$ grep -E -v '^#|^$' httpd.conf |
head
ServerTokens OS
ServerRoot "/etc/httpd"
PidFile run/httpd.pid
Timeout 60
KeepAlive Off
MaxKeepAliveRequests 100
KeepAliveTimeout 15
<IfModule prefork.c>
```

```
StartServers          8

MinSpareServers       5

[jason@www conf]$
```

Use Vim to Edit Files over the Network

```
$ vim scp://remote-host//path/to/file

$ vim scp://remote-user@remote-host//path/to/file
```

If you want to edit a file with vim over SSH, you can let it do the heavy lifting of copying the file back and forth.

```
$ vim scp://linuxserver//home/jason/notes.txt
```

Display Output in a Table

```
$ alias ct='column -t'

$ command | ct
```

Use the column command to format text into multiple columns. By using the -t option, column will count the number of columns the input contains and create a table with that number of columns. This can really make the output of many command easier to read. I find myself using this so often that I created an alias for the command.

```
$ alias ct='column -t'
$ echo -e 'one two\nthree four'
one two
three four
$ echo -e 'one two\nthree four' | ct
one    two
```

```
three four
$ mount -t ext4
/dev/vda2 on / type ext4 (rw)
/dev/vda1 on /boot type ext4 (rw)
$ mount -t ext4 | ct
/dev/vda2  on  /       type  ext4  (rw)
/dev/vda1  on  /boot type  ext4  (rw)
$
```

Grab the Last Word on a Line of Output

```
$ awk '{print $NF}' file
$ cat file | awk '{print $NF}'
```

You can have awk print fields by using $FIELD_NUMBER notation. To print the first field use $1, to print the second use $2, etc. However, if you don't know the number of fields, or don't care to count them, use $NF which represents the total number of fields. Awk separates fields on spaces, but you can use the -F argument to change that behavior. Here is how to print all the shells that are in use on the system. Use a colon as the field separator and then print the last field.

```
$ awk -F: '{print $NF}' /etc/passwd | sort -u
```

If you want to display the shell for each user on the system you can do this.

```
$ awk -F: '{print $1,$NF}' /etc/passwd | sort |
column -t

adm              /sbin/nologin
```

```
apache              /sbin/nologin

avahi-autoipd       /sbin/nologin

bin                 /sbin/nologin

bobb                /bin/bash

. . .
```

View Colorized Output with Less

```
$ ls --color=always | less -R
$ grep --color=always file | less -R
```

Some linux distributions create aliases for ls and grep with the --color=auto option. This causes colors to be used only when the output is going to a terminal. When you pipe the output from ls or grep the color codes aren't emitted. You can force color to always be displayed by ls or grep with --color=always. To have the less command display the raw control characters that create colors, use the -R option.

```
$ grep --color=always -i bob /etc/passwd | less -R
$ ls --color=always -l /etc | less -R
```

Preserve Color When Piping to Grep

```
$ ls -l --color=always | grep --color=never string
```

If you pipe colorized input into grep and grep is an alias with the --color=auto option, grep will discard the color from the input and highlight the string that was grepped for. In order to preserve the colorized input, force grep to not use colors with the --color=never option.

```
$ ls -l --color=always *mp3 | grep --color=never jazz
```

```
-rw-r--r--. 1 jason jason 21267371 Feb 16 11:12 jazz-
album-1.mp3
```

Append Text to a File Using Sudo

```
$ echo text | sudo tee -a file
```

If you have ever tried to append text to a file using redirection following a "sudo echo" command, you quickly find this doesn't work. What happens is the echo statement is executed as root but the redirection occurs as yourself.

```
$ sudo echo "PRODUCTION Environment" >> /etc/motd
-bash: /etc/motd: Permission denied
```

Fortunately, use can use sudo in combination the tee command to append text to a file.

```
$ echo "PRODUCTION Environment" | sudo tee -a
/etc/motd
PRODUCTION Environment
```

Change the Case of a String

```
$ tr [:upper:][:lower:]
$ tr [:lower:][:upper:]
```

When you need to change the case of a string, use the tr command. You can supply ranges to tr like "tr a-z A-Z" or use "tr [:lower:][:upper]".

```
$ ENVIRONMENT=PRODUCTION
```

```
$ DIRECTORY=$(echo $ENVIRONMENT | tr
[:upper:][:lower:])
$ echo $ENVIRONMENT | sudo tee -a /etc/motd
$ tail -1 /etc/motd
PRODUCTION
$ sudo mkdir /var/ww/$DIRECTORY
$ sudo tar zxf wwwfiles.tgz -C /var/ww/$DIRECTORY
```

Display Your Command Search Path in a Human Readable Format

```
$ echo $PATH | tr ':' '\n'
```

Reading a colon separated list of items isn't as easy for us humans as it is for computers. To substitute new lines for colons, use the tr command.

```
$ echo $PATH
/usr/bin:/bin:/usr/local/bin:/bin:/usr/bin:/usr/local
/sbin:/usr/sbin:/sbin
$ echo $PATH | tr ':' '\n'
/usr/bin
/bin
/usr/local/bin
/bin
/usr/bin
/usr/local/sbin
/usr/sbin
/sbin
```

Create a Text File from the Command Line without

Using an Editor

```
$ cat > file
<ctrl-d>
```

If you need to make a quick note and don't need a full blown text editor, you can simply use cat and redirect the output to a file. Press <ctrl-d> when you're finished to create the file.

```
$ cat > shopping.list
eggs
bacon
coffee
<ctrl-d>
$ cat shopping.list
eggs
bacon
coffee
$
```

Display a Block of Text between Two Strings

```
$ awk '/start-pattern/,/stop-pattern/' file.txt
$ command | awk '/start-pattern/,/stop-pattern/'
```

The grep command is great at extracting a single line of text. But what if you need to capture an entire block of text? Use awk and provide it a start and stop pattern. The pattern can simply be a string or even a regular expression.

```
$ sudo dmidecode | awk /Processor/,/Manuf/
```

```
Processor Information
            Socket Designation: SOCKET 0
            Type: Central Processor
            Family: Core i5
            Manufacturer: Intel
$ awk '/worker.c/,/^$/' httpd.conf
<IfModule worker.c>
StartServers            4
MaxClients                  300
MinSpareThreads        25
MaxSpareThreads        75
ThreadsPerChild        25
MaxRequestsPerChild   0
</IfModule>
$
```

Delete a Block of Text between Two Strings

```
$ sed '/start-pattern/,/stop-pattern/d' file
$ command | sed '/start-pattern/,/stop-pattern/d'
file
```

You can delete a block of text with the sed command by providing it a start and stop pattern and telling it to delete that entire range. The patterns can be strings or regular expressions. This example deletes the the first seven lines since "#" matches the first line and "^$" matches the seventh line.

```
$ cat ports.conf
# If you just change the port or add more ports here,
you will likely also
```

```
# have to change the VirtualHost statement in

# /etc/apache2/sites-enabled/000-default

# This is also true if you have upgraded from before
2.2.9-3 (i.e. from

# Debian etch). See /usr/share/doc/apache2.2-
common/NEWS.Debian.gz and

# README.Debian.gz

NameVirtualHost *:80

Listen 80

<IfModule mod_ssl.c>

        # If you add NameVirtualHost *:443 here, you
will also have to change

        # the VirtualHost statement in
/etc/apache2/sites-available/default-ssl

        # to <VirtualHost *:443>

        # Server Name Indication for SSL named
virtual hosts is currently not

        # supported by MSIE on Windows XP.

        Listen 443

</IfModule>

<IfModule mod_gnutls.c>

        Listen 443

</IfModule>

$ sed '/#/,/^$/d' ports.conf

NameVirtualHost *:80

Listen 80

<IfModule mod_ssl.c>

<IfModule mod_gnutls.c>

        Listen 443

</IfModule>
```

Fix Common Typos with Aliases

```
$ alias typo='correct spelling'
```

If you find yourself repeatedly making the same typing mistake over and over, fix it with an alias.

```
$ grpe root /etc/passwd
bash: grpe: command not found
$ echo "alias grpe='grep'" >> ~/.bash_profile
$ . ~/.bash_profile
$ grpe root /etc/passwd
root:x:0:0:root:/root:/bin/bash
$
```

Sort the Body of Output While Leaving the Header on the First Line Intact

Add this function to your personal initialization files such as ~/.bash_profile:

```
body() {
    IFS= read -r header
    printf '%s\n' "$header"
    "$@"
}
$ command | body sort
$ cat file | body sort
```

I find myself wanting to sort the output of commands that contain headers. After the sort is performed the header ends up sorted right along with the rest of the content. This function will keep the header line intact and allow sorting of the remaining lines of output. Here are some examples to illustrate the usage of this function.

```
$ df -h | sort -k 5
/dev/vda2    28G   3.2G  25G         12%    /
tmpfs              504M  68K   504M  1%          /dev/shm
/dev/vda1    485M  444M  17M         97%   /boot
Filesystem  Size  Used  Avail  Use%  Mounted   on
$ df -h | body sort -k 5
Filesystem  Size  Used  Avail  Use%  Mounted   on
/dev/vda2    28G   3.2G  25G         12%    /
tmpfs              504M  68K   504M  1%          /dev/shm
/dev/vda1    485M  444M  17M         97%   /boot
$ ps -eo pid,%cpu,cmd | head -1
  PID %CPU CMD
$ ps -eo pid,%cpu,cmd | sort -nrk2 | head
  675 12.5 mysqld
  PID %CPU CMD
  994  0.0 /usr/sbin/acpid
  963  0.0 /usr/sbin/modem-manager
  958  0.0 NetworkManager
  946  0.0 dbus-daemon
  934  0.0 /usr/sbin/fcoemon --syslog
  931  0.0 [bnx2fc_thread/0]
  930  0.0 [bnx2fc_12_threa]
```

```
929  0.0 [bnx2fc]
$ ps -eo pid,%cpu,cmd | body sort -nrk2 | head
  PID %CPU CMD
  675 12.5 mysqld
  994  0.0 /usr/sbin/acpid
  963  0.0 /usr/sbin/modem-manager
  958  0.0 NetworkManager
  946  0.0 dbus-daemon
  934  0.0 /usr/sbin/fcoemon --syslog
  931  0.0 [bnx2fc_thread/0]
  930  0.0 [bnx2fc_12_threa]
  929  0.0 [bnx2fc]
$
```

Remove a Character or set of Characters from a String or Line of Output

```
$ command | tr -d "X"
$ command | tr -d [SET]
$ cat file | tr -d "X"
$ cat file | tr -d [set]
```

The tr command is typically used to translate characters, but with the -d option it deletes characters. This example shows how to get rid of quotes.

```
$ cat cities.csv
1,"Chicago","USA","IL"
2,"Austin","USA","TX"
3,"Santa Cruz","USA","CA"
```

```
$ cat cities.csv | cut -d, -f2
"Chicago"
"Austin"
"Santa Cruz"
$ cat cities.csv | cut -d, -f2 | tr -d '"'
Chicago
Austin
Santa Cruz
$
```

You can also let tr delete a group of characters. This example removes all the vowels from the output.

```
$ cat cities.csv | cut -d, -f2 | tr -d [aeiou]
"Chcg"
"Astn"
"Snt Crz"
$
```

Count the Number of Occurrences of a String

```
$ uniq -c file
$ command | uniq -c
```

The uniq command omits adjacent duplicate lines from files. Since uniq doesn't examine an entire file or stream of input for unique lines, only unique adjacent lines, it is typically preceded by the sort command via a pipe. You can have the uniq command count the unique occurrences of a string by using the "-c" option. This comes in useful if you are trying to look through log files for occurrences of the same message, PID, status code, username, etc.

Let's find the all of the unique HTTP status codes in an apache web server log file named access.log. To do this, print out the ninth item in the log file with the awk command.

```
$ tail -1 access.log
18.19.20.21 - - [19/Apr/2014:19:51:20 -0400] "GET /
HTTP/1.1" 200 7136 "-" "Mozilla/5.0 (Windows NT 6.1;
WOW64) AppleWebKit/537.36 (KHTML, like Gecko)
Chrome/33.0.1750.154 Safari/537.36"
$ tail -1 access.log | awk '{print $9}'
200
$ awk '{print $9}' access.log | sort | uniq
200
301
302
404
$
```

Let's take it another step forward and count how many of each status code we have.

```
$ awk '{print $9}' access.log | sort | uniq -c | sort
-nr
   5641 200
    207 301
     86 404
     18 302
      2 304
```

$

Now let's see extract the status code and hour from the access.log file and count the unique occurrences of those combinations. Next, lets sort them by number of occurrences. This will show us the hours during which the website was most active.

```
$ cat access.log | awk '{print $9, $4}' | cut -c 1-
4,18-19 | uniq -c | sort -n | tail
      72 200 09
      76 200 06
      81 200 06
      82 200 06
      83 200 06
      83 200 06
      84 200 06
     109 200 20
     122 200 20
     383 200 10
$
```

NETWORKING AND SSH

Serve Files in the Current Directory via a Web Interface

```
$ python -m SimpleHTTPServer
$ python3 -m http.server
```

By default, this command starts a web server and serves up the content in the current directory over port 8000. You can change the port by specifying it at the end of the line. If no index.html file exists in the current directory, then the directory listing is shown. Start the web server and use a web browser to navigate to it. (firefox http://localhost:8000)

This can come in handy when you are working on HTML content and you want to see how it looks in a web browser without installing and configuring a full blown web server.

```
$ python -m SimpleHTTPServer
Serving HTTP on 0.0.0.0 port 8000 …
localhost.localdomain - - [06/Apr/2014 21:49:20] "GET
/ HTTP/1.1" 200 -
```

Here's how to start the web server on the standard HTTP port. Since port 80 is a privileged port, IE it's 1024 or lower, doing this requires root privileges.

```
$ sudo python -m SimpleHTTPServer 80
Serving HTTP on 0.0.0.0 port 80 ...
```

Mount a Directory from a Remote Server on Your Local Host via SSH

```
$ sshfs remote-host:/directory mountpoint
$ fusermount -u mountpiont
```

Sometimes it's easier to work on files and directories if they are, or appear to be, local to your machine. For example, maybe you have a local application that doesn't exist on the server that you use to manipulate files. Instead of downloading the file from the server, modifying it, and and uploading it back to the server, you can mount the remote directory on your local workstation. Here is an example of updating a website over SSH.

```
$ mkdir web-files
$ sshfs www.example.com:/home/jason/public_html
$ bluefish web-files/index.html
$ fusermount -u web-files
```

Just like ssh command, you can use the user@host format if your remote username is different from your local username. Also, if no directory is specified after the colon, then your home directory is assumed.

Get Your Public IP from the Command Line Using Curl

```
$ curl ifconfig.me
```

If you ever need to determine your public (Internet) IP address you can use the ifconfig.me website.

```
$ curl ifconfig.me
198.145.20.140
$ curl ifconfig.me/ip
198.145.20.140
$ curl ifconfig.me/host
pub2.kernel.org
```

SSH into a Remote System without a Password

```
$ ssh-keygen
$ ssh-copy-id remote-host
$ ssh remote-host
```

In order to SSH into a remote host without a password you'll need an SSH key pair consisting of a private and public key. On the remote host the contents of the public key need to be in ~/.ssh/authorized_keys. The ssh-copy-id script performs that work.

If you want to generate a key without a password, simply hit enter when prompted for a passphrase. You can optionally supply a blank string to the -N option. (ssh-keygen -N '')

```
$ ssh-keygen
Generating public/private rsa key pair.
```

Enter file in which to save the key
(/home/jason/.ssh/id_rsa):

Enter passphrase (empty for no passphrase):

Enter same passphrase again:

Your identification has been saved in
/home/jason/.ssh/id_rsa.

Your public key has been saved in
/home/jason/.ssh/id_rsa.pub.

The key fingerprint is:

0d:2e:e4:32:dd:da:60:a5:2e:0f:c5:89:d5:78:30:ad
jason@laptop.localdomain

The key's randomart image is:

```
+--[ RSA 2048]----+
|        o.       |
|         =.      |
|        +.=      |
|       BEB o     |
|      + @ S .    |
|       * =       |
|      o o .      |
|       +         |
|        .        |
+-----------------+
```

$ ssh-copy-id linuxserver

jason@192.168.122.60's password:

Now try logging into the machine, with "ssh
'linuxserver'", and check in:

   .ssh/authorized_keys

to make sure we haven't added extra keys that you
weren't expecting.

```
$ ssh linuxserver
$ hostname
linuxserver
$
```

Show Open Network Connections

```
$ sudo lsof -Pni
```

The lsof command can not only be used to display open files, but open network ports, and network connections. The -P option prevents the conversion of port numbers to port names. The -n option prevents the conversion of IP addresses to host names. The -i option tells lsof to display network connections.

```
$ sudo lsof -Pni
```

COMMAND	PID	USER	FD	TYPE	DEVICE	SIZE/OFF
NODE NAME						
dhclient	989	root		6u	IPv4	11522
0t0 UDP *:68						
sshd	1202	root		3u	IPv4	12418
0t0 TCP *:22 (LISTEN)						
sshd	1202	root		4u	IPv6	12423
0t0 TCP *:22 (LISTEN)						
ntpd	1210	ntp	16u	IPv4	12464	
0t0 UDP *:123						
ntpd	1210	ntp	17u	IPv6	12465	
0t0 UDP *:123						
ntpd	1210	ntp	18u	IPv4	12476	
0t0 UDP 127.0.0.1:123						
ntpd	1210	ntp	19u	IPv4	12477	
0t0 UDP 192.168.122.60:123						

```
ntpd            1210    ntp    20u   IPv6   12478
0t0    UDP  [::1]:123

ntpd            1210    ntp    21u   IPv6   12479
0t0    UDP  [fe80::5054:ff:fe52:d858]:123

master          1364    root   12u   IPv4   12761
0t0    TCP  127.0.0.1:25  (LISTEN)

clock-app 12174 jason   21u   IPv4   78889           0t0
TCP  192.168.122.60:39021->184.25.102.40:80
(ESTABLISHED)

sshd            12339   root         3r    IPv4   74023
0t0    TCP  192.168.122.60:22->192.168.122.1:34483
(ESTABLISHED)

sshd            12342   jason        3u    IPv4   74023
0t0    TCP  192.168.122.60:22->192.168.122.1:34483
(ESTABLISHED)

$
```

Compare the Differences between a Remote and Local File

```
$ ssh remote-host cat /path/to/remotefile | diff
/path/to/localfile -
```

To display the differences between a local and remote file, cat a file over ssh and pipe the output into a diff or sdiff command. The diff and sdiff commands can accept standard input in lieu of a file by supplying it a dash for one of the file names.

```
$ ssh linuxsvr cat /etc/passwd | diff /etc/passwd -
32c32
< terry:x:503:1000::/home/terry:/bin/ksh

---

> terry:x:503:1000::/home/terry:/bin/bash
```

```
35a36
> bob:x:1000:1000:Bob Smith:/home/bob:/bin/bash
$
```

Send Email from the Command Line

```
$ mail recipient@domain.com
$ echo 'message' | mail -s 'subject'
recipient@domain.com
```

To send an email use the mail command. You can enter in a message interactively or via a pipe. End your interactive message with ctrl-d.

```
$ mail jim@mycorp.com
Subject: Message from the command line
Isn't this great?

EOT

$ echo "Here's the lazy way" | mail -s 'Message from
the command line' jim@mycorp.com
```

Send an Email Attachment from the Command Line

```
$ mail -a /path/to/attachment
$ echo 'message' | mail -s 'subject' -a
/path/to/attachment recipient@domain.com
```

If you ever need to send an email attachment from the command line, use the -a option to the mail command.

```
$ echo "Here is the file you requested" | mail -s
"The file" -a /tmp/files.tgz jim@mycorp.com
$
```

Create an SSH Tunnel to Access Remote Resources

```
$ ssh -N -L local-port:host:remote-port remote-host
```

To create an SSH tunnel, use the -L option. The first port is the port that will be opened on your local machine. Connections to this port will be tunneled through remote-host and sent to the host and remote port specified in the -L option. The -N option tells SSH to not execute a command -- your shell -- on the remote host.

Let's say you want to access a website that isn't available on the internet, but is accessible from a server that you have SSH access to. You can create a tunnel that allows you to browse that website like you were behind the company's firewall. This command will forward any connections from your local machine on port 8000 through the jump server to the intranet server on port 80. Point your web browser to http://localhost:8000 and start surfing.

```
$ ssh -N -L 8000:intranet.acme.com:80 jump-server &
[1] 23253
$ firefox http://localhost:8000
```

Another use case is to access a service that is running on a server that you have SSH access to. If you need access to a mysql server that only allows database connections from specific hosts, you can create an SSH tunnel for your connection. Since the mysql service is running on localhost:3306 of the remote machine, the -L option would look like this: -L 3306:localhost:3306. You can use the mysql command line client on your local machine to connect to the database, but what's even more interesting is to use graphical desktop applications that aren't available on the server. For example, you could use this tunnel and connect to the database with MySQL Workbench, Navicat, or some other application.

```
$ ssh -N -L 3306:localhost:3306 db01 &

[1] 13455

$ mysql -h 127.0.0.1

Welcome to the MySQL monitor.  Commands end with ; or
\g.

Your MySQL connection id is 9

Server version: 5.1.73 Source distribution

Copyright (c) 2000, 2013, Oracle and/or its
affiliates. All rights reserved.

Oracle is a registered trademark of Oracle
Corporation and/or its

affiliates. Other names may be trademarks of their
respective

owners.

Type 'help;' or '\h' for help. Type '\c' to clear the
current input statement.

mysql>
```

Find out Which Programs Are Listening on Which Ports

```
$ sudo netstat -nutlp
```

Here are the descriptions of the netstat options used in order to get a
list of programs and the ports that they are listening on.

-n show numerical addresses instead of determining symbolic names
-u include the UDP protocol
-t include the TCP protocol
-l show only listening sockets
-p show the PID and program name

```
$  sudo netstat -nutlp

Active Internet connections (only servers)

Proto Recv-Q Send-Q Local Address  Foreign Address
State    PID/Program name

tcp            0          0  0.0.0.0:3306
0.0.0.0:*       LISTEN  4546/mysqld

tcp            0          0  0.0.0.0:22
0.0.0.0:*       LISTEN  1161/sshd

tcp            0          0  127.0.0.1:25
0.0.0.0:*       LISTEN  1325/master

tcp            0          0  :::80          :::*
LISTEN   4576/httpd

tcp            0          0  :::22          :::*
LISTEN   1161/sshd

udp            0          0  0.0.0.0:68
0.0.0.0:*                1008/dhclient

$
```

Use a Different SSH Key for a given Remote Host

Put the following in the ~/.ssh/config file.

```
Host remote-host

IdentityFile ~/.ssh/id_rsa-remote-host
```

If you need or want to use different SSH keys for different hosts, you can explicitly specify them on the command line with the -i option to ssh.

```
$ ssh -i ~/.ssh/id_rsa-db1 db1.example.com
```

If you want to forego specifying the key each time you can create an entry in your ~/.ssh/config file and specify the key there.

```
$ cat ~/.ssh/config
```

```
Host db1.example.com
        IdentityFile ~/.ssh/id_rsa-db1
$ ssh db1.example.com
```

You can use wildcards in the host specification.

```
$ cat~/.ssh/config
Host db*
        IdentityFile ~/.ssh/id_rsa-db1
Host *.work.net
        IdentityFile ~/work-files/keys/id_rsa
$ ssh jim@jumpbox.work.net
```

If you name your SSH keys after the fully qualified domain names of the hosts they relate to, you can use the %h escape character to simplify your ~/.ssh/config file. Instead of having a host entry for each and every server, the %h syntax expands to the fully qualified domain name of the host your are connecting to.

```
$ cat ~/.ssh/config
Host *.example.com
IdentityFile ~/.ssh/id_rsa-%h
$ ls -1 ~/.ssh/id_rsa-*
id_rsa-lax-db-01.example.com
id_rsa-lax-db-01.example.com.pub
id_rsa-lax-web-01.example.com
id_rsa-lax-web-01.example.com.pub
$ ssh lax-db-01.example.com
```

Avoid Having to Type Your Username When Connecting via SSH

Put the following in the ~/.ssh/config file.

```
Host remote-host
User username
```

If you have a different username on your local Linux machine than you do on the remote linux machine, you have to specify it when connecting via SSH. It looks like this.

```
$ ssh jim@server1.example.com
```

To avoid having to type "username@" each time, add a host entry to your ~/.ssh/config file.

```
Host server1.example.com
        User jim
```

Once your have configured the host entry, you can simply ssh into the remote host.

```
$ whoami
james
$ ssh server1.example.com
$ whoami
jim
$
```

Simplify Multi-Hop SSH Connections and Transparently Proxy SSH Connections

Put the following in the ~/.ssh/config file.

```
Host jumphost.example.com
   ProxyCommand none
Host *.example.com
   ProxyCommand ssh -W %h:%p jumphost.example.com
```

If you need to access a host that sits behind an SSH gateway server or jump server, you can make your life easier by telling SSH to automatically use the SSH gateway when you connect to the final remote host. Instead of first connecting to the gateway and then entering another ssh command to connect to the destination host, you simply type "ssh destination-host" from your local machine. Using the above configuration, this command will proxy your ssh connection to server1 through jumphost.

```
$ ssh server1.example.com
$ uname -n
server1
$
```

Disconnect from a Remote Session and Reconnect at a Later Time, Picking up Where You Left Off

```
$ ssh remote-host
$ screen
ctrl-a, d
$ exit
```

```
$ ssh remote-host
$ screen -r
```

When I have a long running process that I need to complete on a remote host, I always start a screen session before launching that process. I don't want a blip in my network connection to interrupt the work being performed on the remote host. Sometimes I launch a process, detach from the session, and reconnect later to examine all the output that occurred while I was away.

First, ssh into the remote host. Next, start a screen session. Start performing your work on the remote host. Detach from the screen session by typing ctrl-a followed by d. The process you started will still be running in the screen session while you're away. Also, any output generated will be available for you to view at a later time.

```
$ ssh remote-host
$ screen
$ /usr/local/bin/migrate-db
Starting DB migration at Sun Apr 13 21:02:50 EDT 2014
<ctrl-a,d>
[detached]
$ exit
```

To reconnect to your screen session, connect to the remote host and type screen -r. If there is any output that scrolled past the top of the screen, you can view by typing ctrl-a followed by the escape key. Now use the vi navigation key bindings to view the output history. For example, you can type k to move up one line or ctrl-b to page up. Once you are finished looking at the output history, hit escape to return to the live session. To quit your screen session, type exit.

```
$ ssh remote-host
$ screen -r
Starting DB migration at 21:02
table1 migrated at 21:34
table2 migrated at 22:11
table3 migrated at 22:54
DB migration completed at 23:04
$ exit
[screen is terminating]
$ exit
```

Screen is one of the most widely used and readily available screen multiplexers. However, there are alternatives such as tmux, dtach, and byobu.

Configure SSH to Append Domain Names to Host Names Based on a Pattern

The contents of ~/.ssh/config:

```
host-prefix* !*.domain.com
        HostName %h.domain.com
```

If you connect to hosts in multiple domains via ssh it can get tiresome typing out the fully qualified domain name each time. One way around this problem is to add each domain to the search list in /etc/resolv.conf. The resolver will the attempt the resolution for the specified host name in each of the domains in the search list until it finds one that resolves.

```
$ cat /etc/resolv.conf
```

```
nameserver 8.8.8.8

nameserver 8.8.4.4

search domain1.com domain2.com domain3.com
domain4.com domain5.com domain6.com domain7.com
```

When typing "ssh remote-host" with the above resolv.conf in place, the resolver will attempt to translate remote-host.domain1.com into an IP address. If that fails, it will attempt to resolve remote-host.domain2.com, etc. The problem with the above reslov.conf is that the search list is limited to just six domains. So, remote-host.domain7.com is never attempted. Additionally, the search list is limited to 256 characters, regardless the number of domains.

How can you get around the six domain search list limit? If you're lucky enough to have a pattern of hostnames that correlate with domain names, you can configure ssh to do the resolution. For example, for FQDNs like "ny-www1.newyork.company.com" and "ny-mysql-07.newyork.company.com" you can create a rule that appends ".newyork.company.com" to any host that begins with "ny." You'll also want to tell ssh to ignore any hosts that begin with "ny" that already have ".newyork.company.com" appended to them. Here's an example ~/.ssh/config file that does that.

```
$ cat ~/.ssh/config

ny* !*.newyork.company.com

        HostName %h.newyork.company.com

db* !*.databases.company.com

        HostName %h.databases.company.com

jump* !*.company.com

        HostName %h.company.com
```

Now when you type "ssh ny-test" ssh will attempt to connect to "ny-test.newyork.company.com." For hosts that begin with "db," ssh will append ".databases.company.com" to the host name. Hosts the begin with "jump" will have the ".company.com" domain name appened to them.

```
$ ssh ny-www1
$ hostname -f
ny-www1.newyork.company.com
$ exit
$ ssh jump-ny-01
$ hostname -f
jump-ny-01.company.com
$ exit
$
```

Run a Command Immune to Hangups, Allowing the Job to Run after You Disconnect

```
$ nohup command &
```

Normally when you start a job in the background and log out of your session the job gets killed. One way to ensure a command keeps running after you disconnect from the host is to use the nohup command. No hup stands for no hang up. By default the output of the command is stored in a file named "nohup.out" in the directory the program was launched in. You can examine the contents of this file later to see the output of the command. To use a different filename, employ redirection.

```
$ ssh db-server
```

```
$ nohup /usr/local/bin/upgradedb.sh  &
[1] 13370
$ exit
$ ssh db-server
$ cat nohup.out
Starting database upgrade.
...
Database upgrade complete.
$ nohup /usr/local/bin/post-upgrade.sh >
/tmp/post.log &
[1] 16711
$ exit
$ ssh db-server
$ cat /tmp/post.log
Post processing completed.
$
```

Encrypt Your Web Browsing Data with an SSH SOCKS Proxy

```
$ ssh -D PORT remote-host
```

If you are using an open wireless hotspot and want to ensure your web browsing data is encrypted, you can redirect your web browsing traffic through another host via SSH. Start ssh with the "-D" option and provide a port to open up on your local computer for proxy connections. If you only want to perform the port forwarding and not actually log into the shell of the remote host, use the "-N" option for ssh. Configure your web browser to use a SOCKS 5 proxy using localhost for the host and the port you supplied to ssh.

```
$ ssh -ND 1080 ubuntu@ec2-75-101-157-145.compute-
1.amazonaws.com

$ firefox http://www.mybank.com
```

Download a Webpage, HTTP Data, or Use a Web API from the Command Line

```
$ curl -o file.html http://website/webpage

$ wget http://website/webpage
```

The curl and wget commands can be used to download a webpage or anything that is available on a web server. You can use these commands to interact with HTTP APIs, download software packages, download a status page, or even get the current weather.

Here's an example of checking the status page of your local apache web server.

```
$ curl -o server-status.html http://localhost/server-status
  % Total    % Received % Xferd  Average Speed   Time          Time
                                 Time   Current
                                 Dload  Upload
Total     Spent         Left  Speed
100  6148  100  6148        0        0  1070k
0 --:--:-- --:--:-- --:--:-- 1200k
$ wget http://localhost/server-status
--2014-04-19 14:37:18--  http://localhost/server-status
Resolving localhost (localhost)... 127.0.0.1
Connecting to localhost (localhost)|127.0.0.1|:80...
connected.
HTTP request sent, awaiting response... 200 OK
```

```
Length: 6377 (6.2K) [text/html]

Saving to: `server-status'

100%[=====>] 6,377              --.-K/s    in 0s

2014-04-19 14:37:18 (105 MB/s) - `server-status'
saved [6377/6377]
$ grep uptime server-status*

server-status:<dt>Server uptime:   50 minutes 13
seconds</dt>

server-status.html:<dt>Server uptime:   50 minutes 5
seconds</dt>
```

Here's an example of getting the current weather.

```
$ curl -so lax-weather.html \

http://weather.noaa.gov/pub/data/observations/metar/d
ecoded/KLAX.TXT

$ cat lax-weather.html

LOS ANGELES INTERNTL AIRPORT, CA, United States
(KLAX) 33-56N 118-23W 46M

Apr 19, 2014 - 02:53 PM EDT / 2014.04.19 1853 UTC

Wind: from the W (260 degrees) at 10 MPH (9 KT):0

Visibility: 10 mile(s):0

Sky conditions: mostly cloudy

Temperature: 64.9 F (18.3 C)

Dew Point: 54.0 F (12.2 C)

Relative Humidity: 67%

Pressure (altimeter): 30.03 in. Hg (1016 hPa)

ob: KLAX 191853Z 26009KT 10SM FEW022 BKN220 18/12
A3003 RMK AO2 SLP167 T01830122

cycle: 19
```

```
$ wget -q \

http://weather.noaa.gov/pub/data/observations/metar/d
ecoded/KLAX.TXT

$ cat KLAX.TXT

LOS ANGELES INTERNTL AIRPORT, CA, United States
(KLAX) 33-56N 118-23W 46M

Apr 19, 2014 - 02:53 PM EDT / 2014.04.19 1853 UTC

Wind: from the W (260 degrees) at 10 MPH (9 KT):0

Visibility: 10 mile(s):0

Sky conditions: mostly cloudy

Temperature: 64.9 F (18.3 C)

Dew Point: 54.0 F (12.2 C)

Relative Humidity: 67%

Pressure (altimeter): 30.03 in. Hg (1016 hPa)

ob: KLAX 191853Z 26009KT 10SM FEW022 BKN220 18/12
A3003 RMK AO2 SLP167 T01830122

cycle: 19
$
```

Download and install a package.

```
$ wget -q \

https://download.elasticsearch.org/elasticsearch/elas
ticsearch/elasticsearch-1.1.1.deb

$ sudo dpkg -i elasticsearch-1.1.1.deb

Selecting previously unselected package
elasticsearch.

(Reading database ... 162097 files and directories
currently installed.)

Unpacking elasticsearch (from elasticsearch-
```

```
1.1.1.deb) ...

Setting up elasticsearch (1.1.1) ...

Adding system user `elasticsearch' (UID 116) ...

Adding new user `elasticsearch' (UID 116) with group
`elasticsearch' ...

Not creating home directory
`/usr/share/elasticsearch'.

### NOT starting elasticsearch by default on bootup,
please execute

 sudo update-rc.d elasticsearch defaults 95 10

### In order to start elasticsearch, execute

 sudo /etc/init.d/elasticsearch start

Processing triggers for ureadahead ...

$ sudo /etc/init.d/elasticsearch start

 * Starting Elasticsearch Server
[ OK ]
$
```

Interact with a web API.

```
$ curl http://localhost:9200
{
  "status" : 200,
  "name" : "NFL Superpro",
  "version" : {
        "number" : "1.1.1",
        "build_hash" : "f1585f096d3f3985e73456dcc",
        "build_timestamp" : "2014-04-16T14:27:12Z",
        "build_snapshot" : false,
```

```
        "lucene_version" : "4.7"
  },
  "tagline" : "You Know, for Search"
}
$ curl http://localhost:9200/_cluster/health?pretty
{
  "cluster_name" : "elasticsearch",
  "status" : "green",
  "timed_out" : false,
  "number_of_nodes" : 1,
  "number_of_data_nodes" : 1,
  "active_primary_shards" : 0,
  "active_shards" : 0,
  "relocating_shards" : 0,
  "initializing_shards" : 0,
  "unassigned_shards" : 0
}
$
```

Use Vim to Edit Files over the Network

```
$ vim scp://remote-host//path/to/file
$ vim scp://remote-user@remote-host//path/to/file
```

If you want to edit a file with vim over SSH, you can let it do the heavy lifting of copying the file back and forth.

```
$ vim scp://linuxserver//home/jason/notes.txt
```

SHELL SCRIPTING

Use a for Loop at the Command Line

```
$ for VAR in LIST
> do
>   # use $VAR
> done
```

When you need to perform the same action for a list of items, you can use a for loop right from your shell.

```
$ for USER in bob jill fred
> do
>   sudo passwd -l $USER
>   logger -t naughty-user $USER
> done
Locking password for user bob.
passwd: Success
Locking password for user jill.
passwd: Success
```

```
Locking password for user fred.
passwd: Success
$ sudo tail -3 /var/log/messages
Apr  8 19:29:03 linuxserver naughty-user: bob
Apr  8 19:29:03 linuxserver naughty-user: jill
Apr  8 19:29:03 linuxserver naughty-user: fred
```

You can also type entire loop on one command line

```
$ for USER in bob jill fred; do sudo passwd -l $USER;
logger -t naughty-user $USER; done
. . .
```

Command Substitution

```
$ VAR=`command`
$ VAR=$(command)
```

There are two forms of command substitution. The first form uses backticks (`) to surround a command while the second form uses a dollar sign followed by parenthesis that surround a command. They are functionally equivalent with the backtick form being the older style. The output of the command can be used as an argument to another command, to set a variable, or for generating the argument list for a for loop.

```
$ EXT_FILESYSTEMS=$(grep ext fstab |awk '{print $2}')
$ echo $EXT_FILESYSTEMS
/ /boot
$ cp file.txt file.txt.`date +%F`
```

```
$ ls file.txt*

file.txt   file.txt.2014-04-08

$ ps -fp $(cat /var/run/ntpd.pid)

UID             PID  PPID  C STIME TTY              TIME
CMD

ntp            1210        1  0 Apr06 ?
00:00:05 ntpd -u ntp:ntp -p /var/run/ntpd

$ sudo kill -9 $(cat /var/run/ntpd.pid)

$ for x in $(cut -d: -f1 /etc/passwd); do groups $x;
done

jason : jason sales

bobdjr : sales

jim : jim
```

Store Command Line Output as a Variable to Use Later

```
$ for VAR in LIST

> do

>   VAR2=$(command)

>   VAR3=$(command)

>   echo "$VAR2 VAR3"

> done
```

Command substitution can be used to assign values to variables. If you need to reuse the output of a command multiple times, assign it to a variable once and reuse the variable. This example shows how the output of the id command is used multiple times in one script.

```
$ for USER in $(cut -f1 -d: /etc/passwd)

> do

>   UID_MIN=$(grep ^UID_MIN /etc/login.defs | awk
```

```
'{print $NF}')
>   USERID=$(id -u $USER)
>   [ $USERID -lt $UID_MIN ] || {
>         echo "Forcing password expiration for $USER
with UID of $USERID."
>         sudo passwd -e $USER
>   }
> done
```

Forcing password expiration for bob with UID of 1000.

Forcing password expiration for bobdjr with UID of 1001.

Forcing password expiration for bobh with UID of 1002.

Read in Input One Line at a Time

```
$ while read LINE
> do
>    # Do something with $LINE
> done < file.txt
$ command | while read LINE
> do
>    # Do something with $LINE
> done
```

If you want to iterate over a list of words, use a for loop. If you want to iterate over a line, use a while loop in combination with a read statement and redirection.

Let's look for file systems that are over 90% utilized. If we try to use an if statement it will break up the output into word chunks like this.

```
$ df | head -1
Filesystem 1K-blocks Used Available Use% Mounted on
$ for x in $(df)
> do
> echo $x
> done
Filesystem
1K-blocks
Used
Available
Use%
Mounted
on
...
```

We need to read in entire lines at a time like this.

```
$ df | while read LINE
> do
> echo $LINE
> done
Filesystem 1K-blocks Used Available Use% Mounted on
...
```

Here is one way to find file systems that are over 90% utilized.

```
$ df
Filesystem 1K-blocks Used Available Use% Mounted on
/dev/sda2   28891260 3270340      25327536   12% /
tmpfs          515320       72      515248    1% /dev/shm
/dev/sda1      495844   453683        16561   97% /boot
$ df | grep [0-9]% | while read LINE
> do
>    use=$(echo $LINE | awk '{print $5}' | tr -d '%')
>    mountpoint=$(echo $LINE | awk '{print $6}')
> [ $use -gt 90 ] && echo "$mountpoint is over 90%
utilized."
> done
/boot is over 90% utilized.
$
```

Instead of assigning variables within the while loop, you can assign them with the read statement. Here is how this method looks.

```
$ df | grep [0-9]% | while read fs blocks used
available use mountpoint
> do
>    use=$(echo $use | tr -d '%')
>    [ $use -gt 90 ] && echo "$mountpoint is over 90%
utilized."
> done
/boot is over 90% utilized.
```

Accept User Input and Store It in a Variable

```
$ read VAR
```

```
$ read -n 1 VAR

$ read -p "Prompt text" VAR
```

To accept user input from a user, use the read command. Read will accept an entire line of input and store it into a variable. You can force read to only read a limited number of characters by using the -n option. Instead of using echo statements before a read command, you can supply a prompt by using the -p option. Here is a sample script that uses these techniques.

The contents of backup.sh:

```
#!/bin/bash

while true

do

   read -p "What server would you like to backup? "
SERVER

   echo "Backing up $SERVER"

   /usr/local/bin/backup $SERVER

   read -p "Backup another server? (y/n) " -n 1
BACKUP_AGAIN

   echo

   [ "$BACKUP_AGAIN" = "y" ] || break

done
```

```
$ ./backup.sh

What server would you like to backup? thor

Backing up thor

Backup another server? (y/n) y
```

```
What server would you like to backup? loki
Backing up loki
Backup another server? (y/n) n
$
```

Sum All the Numbers in a given Column of a Text

```
$ awk '{ sum += $1 } END { print sum }' file
$ cat file| awk '{ sum += $1 } END { print sum }
```

Awk can be used to tally up a column of values. You can use this trick to add up all the disk space used across all the file systems on a given system, for example.

```
$ df -mt ext4
Filesystem 1M-blocks Used Available Use% Mounted on
/dev/sda2   28215   3285         24644   12% /
/dev/sda1     485     55           406   12% /boot
$ df -mt ext4 | awk '{ sum += $3 } END {print sum}'
3340
$ sudo dmidecode --type memory
          Size: No Module Installed
          Size: 4096 MB
          Size: No Module Installed
          Size: 4096 MB
$ sudo dmidecode --type memory | grep 'Size:' | awk
'{sum+=$2} END {print sum}'
8192
$
```

Automatically Answer Yes to Any Command

```
$ yes | command
$ yes "string" | command
```

If you are trying to automate a process that requires user input, check out the yes command. By default yes simply prints out "y" until it is killed. You can make yes repeat any string. If you wanted to automatically answer "no" you could run "yes no."

```
$ ./install-my-app.sh
Are you sure you want to install my-app? (y/n) y
Ok, my-app installed.
$ yes | ./install-my-app.sh
Ok, my-app installed.
$
```

SYSTEM ADMINISTRATION

Display Mounted File Systems in a Tabular Format

```
$ mount | column -t
```

The output of the mount command is not formatted in an easy-to-read manner. To make each column line up, pipe the output of the mount command to "column -t". By default mount displays all mounted filesystems, even the pseudo-filesystems like /proc and /sys. To limit output to a filesystem type, use the -t option and provide a type.

```
$ mount -t ext4
/dev/mapper/sys-lv_root  on / type  ext4  (rw)
/dev/sda1 on  /boot  type  ext4  (rw)
$ mount -t ext4 | column -t
/dev/mapper/sys-lv_root on  /      type ext4 (rw)
/dev/sda1                   on  /boot type ext4 (rw)
```

Kill All Processes for a given User or Program

```
$ pkill -9 command
$ pkill -9 -u user command
```

If you need to kill several processes with the same command, use the pkill command. If you only want to kill processes for a given user, use the -u option. Pkill will only kill the processes when all the criteria match. That means you can kill all of a given process that is being run by a specific user.

```
$ ps -ef| grep http | grep -v grep
root          12253          1  0 10:55 ?
00:00:00 /usr/sbin/httpd

apache    12255 12253  0 10:55 ?              00:00:00
/usr/sbin/httpd

apache    12256 12253  0 10:55 ?              00:00:00
/usr/sbin/httpd

apache    12257 12253  0 10:55 ?              00:00:00
/usr/sbin/httpd

apache    12258 12253  0 10:55 ?              00:00:00
/usr/sbin/httpd

apache    12259 12253  0 10:55 ?              00:00:00
/usr/sbin/httpd

apache    12260 12253  0 10:55 ?              00:00:00
/usr/sbin/httpd

apache    12261 12253  0 10:55 ?              00:00:00
/usr/sbin/httpd

apache    12262 12253  0 10:55 ?              00:00:00
/usr/sbin/httpd
```

```
$ sudo pkill -9 httpd

$ ps -ef| grep http | grep -v grep

$ ps -ef| grep ssh | grep -v grep

root            1202        1  0 Apr06 ?
00:00:00 /usr/sbin/sshd

root          12339  1202  0 11:22 ?
00:00:00 sshd: jason [priv]

jason         12342 12339  0 11:22 ?
00:00:00 sshd: jason@pts/0

root          12368  1202  1 11:23 ?
00:00:00 sshd: bob [priv]

bob           12372 12368  0 11:23 ?
00:00:00 sshd: bob@pts/1

$ sudo killall -u bob sshd

$ ps -ef| grep ssh | grep -v grep

root            1202        1  0 Apr06 ?
00:00:00 /usr/sbin/sshd

root          12339  1202  0 11:22 ?
00:00:00 sshd: jason [priv]

jason         12342 12339  0 11:22 ?
00:00:00 sshd: jason@pts/0

$
```

Repeat a Command until It Succeeds

```
$ while true

> do

>   command && break

> done
```

The while loop will continue until the condition is false or it encounters a break. In his case we effectively create an infinite loop and break once our chosen command succeeds. If you want to keep pinging a host until it responds, you could use this while loop.

```
$ while true
> do
>    ping -c1 -W1 remote-host >/dev/null 2>&1 && break
> done ; echo "Remote-host is up at $(date)."
Remote-host is up at Fri Apr 11 21:30:29 EDT 2014.
$
```

If you're waiting for a file to show up on your server, you could use this while loop.

```
$ while true
> do
>    ls /svr/ftp/incoming/payroll.txt.gpg 2>/dev/null && break
> done; echo "Payroll file arrived at $(date)."
Payroll file arrived at Fri Apr 11 21:33:23 EDT 2014.
```

Find Who Is Using the Most Disk Space

```
$ sudo du -s /home | sort -n
```

This command will display the person who is using the most disk space in their home directory. The users will little disk space will be displayed at the top of your screen and the users using the most disk space will be displayed at the bottom.

```
$ sudo du -s /home/* | sort -n
32      /home/pat
32      /home/terry
40      /home/jim
40      /home/jimbob
44      /home/oracle
19184      /home/adminuser
22208      /home/bob
65132      /home/jason
$
```

If you are looking for a more graphical way to display disk usage, check out the neat utility ncdu.

```
$ ncdu /home
ncdu 1.10 ~ Use the arrow keys to navigate, press ?
for help
--- /home -------------------------------
37.9GiB [#########] /ryan
 1.3MiB [                    ] /lucas
Total disk usage:  37.9GiB  Apparent size:  37.8GiB
Items: 156055
```

Find the Files That Are Using the Most Disk Space

```
$ find / -type f -exec wc -c {} \; | sort -n
```

Use find to execute the "wc -c" command against each file, revealing it's size in bytes, and then sort that output. The smallest files will be displayed first, and the largest files will be displayed last. If you are scanning every file on a system, this command could take awhile to complete.

```
$ sudo find /var -xdev -type f -exec wc -c {} \; |
sort -n
0 /var/cache/apt/archives/lock
...
2572437 /var/lib/dpkg/available-old
2573098 /var/lib/dpkg/available
38433001 /var/cache/apt/pkgcache.bin
39872802 49659904 /var/cache/apt-xapian-
index/index.1/termlist.DB
62783488 /var/cache/apt-xapian-
index/index.1/postlist.DB
$
```

List Processes, Sorted by Memory Usage

```
$ ps aux | sort -nk 4
```

Use this command to find the processes that are consuming the most memory. The processes using the least amount of memory will scroll off the top of your screen and the ones consuming the most amount of memory will be just above your shell prompt.

In this example, mysqld is consuming 1.3% of the memory on this host.

```
$ ps aux| head -1
USER   PID  %CPU %MEM       VSZ   RSS  TTY    STAT
START   TIME COMMAND
$ ps aux | sort -nk 4 | tail -5
```

```
root   2969   0.0   0.3   11856   3228 ?      Ss   17:16
0:00 sshd: jason [priv]

root   4576   0.0   0.3   11364   3380 ?      Ss   17:52
0:00 /usr/sbin/httpd

root    958   0.0   0.3   20844   4084 ?      Ssl  00:00
0:00 NetworkManager

68     1003   0.0   0.4   17104   4268 ?      Ssl  00:00
0:00 hald

mysql 4546   0.0   1.3 136332 13848 pts/0 Sl  17:52
0:01 /usr/libexec/mysqld

$
```

List Processes, Sorted by CPU Usage

```
$ ps aux | sort -nk 3
```

Use this command to find the processes that are consuming the most CPU. The processes using the least amount of CPU will scroll off the top of your screen and the ones consuming the most amount of CPU will be just above your shell prompt.

In this example, mysqld is consuming 94% of the CPU on this host.

```
$ ps aux| head -1
USER   PID   %CPU %MEM        VSZ    RSS  TTY    STAT
START   TIME COMMAND
$ ps aux | sort -nk 4 | tail -5
root   2469   0.0   0.3   11856     3228 ?      Ss   17:16
0:00 /usr/sbin/fcoemon

root    452   0.0   0.3   20844     4084 ?      Ssl  00:00
0:00 master

root   5571   2.1   0.3   11364     3380 ?      Ss   17:52
0:00 /usr/sbin/httpd
```

```
mysql 4447  94 12.8 2134672 1031064 ?    Sl   10:52
27:39 /usr/libexec/mysqld
$
```

Quickly Tell If You Are on a 32 Bit or 64 Bit System

```
$ getconf LONG_BIT
```

If you're on a system and need to know if it's 32 or 64 bit, use getconf.

```
$ getconf LONG_BIT
32
$ ssh remote-host getconf LONG_BIT
64
```

Generate a Random Password

```
$ openssl rand -base64 48 | cut -c1-PASSWORD_LENGTH
$ gpw () {  openssl rand -base64 48 | cut -c1-${1}; }
```

You can use the openssl command to generate a random password. If you find yourself doing this often, you can create a function. Simply pass in how long you want the password to be.

```
$ echo 'gpw () {openssl rand -base64 48|cut -c1-${1};
}' >> ~/.bash_profile
$ . ~/.bash_profile
$ gpw
t3eyxkXBHAzb3VdR7G8NV3fMvZpXLOvT+AQwgQnw9pLm/UaRNHcPB
jKaQsr26i3k
$ gpw 6
uu1ZMb
```

FILES AND DIRECTORIES

Quickly Make a Backup of a File

```
$ cp file{,.bak}
```

You can use brace expansion to quickly create a backup copy of a file. Brace expansion allows you to create multiple command line arguments from a single argument. The single argument is combined with all the strings that are given within the braces and creates as many new arguments as brace strings. Values in the braces can either be comma separated strings or a sequence expression. Examples of sequence expressions include {1..5} and {a..z}.

```
$ sudo cp /etc/passwd{,.bak}
$ ls /etc/passwd*
/etc/passwd   /etc/passwd.bak
$ mkdir -p ~/my-app/{bin,lib,log}
$ ls ~/my-app/
bin   lib   log
$ echo 10.0.0.{0..7}
10.0.0.0 10.0.0.1 10.0.0.2 10.0.0.3 10.0.0.4 10.0.0.5
```

10.0.0.6 10.0.0.7

Quickly Change a File's Extension

```
$ mv file{.old,.new}
```

To rename a file with a new extension employ brace expansion. This example changes a ".txt" file to a ".doc" file.

```
$ ls report*
report.txt
$ mv report.{txt,doc}
$ ls report*
report.doc
$
```

Here's another example.

```
$ ls httpd*
httpd.cfg
$ mv httpd.{cfg,conf}
$ ls httpd*
httpd.conf
$
```

This command will add an extension to a file.

```
$ ls jazz*
jazz
```

```
$ mv jazz{,.mp3}
$ ls jazz*
jazz.mp3
$
```

Create Backups of Files by Date with Ease

```
$ alias d='date +%F'
```

By using the date format of YYYY-MM-DD for file or directory names, you make ls output more human friendly. You can quickly tell the date order of the files when using this format.

```
$ ls -1 file*
file.2013-04-08
file.2013-12-21
file.2014-04-08
$ ls -1 other-file.*
other-file.04-08-2013
other-file.04-08-2014
other-file.12-21-2013
```

Before making a change to a file I like to make a backup copy of it. I also like to know when I made the backup. By creating an alias of "d" which is short for the date in YYYY-MM-DD format, I can quickly create these types of backups.

```
$ echo "alias d='date +%F'" >> ~/.bash_profile
$ ~/.bash_profile
$ d
```

```
2014-04-08
$ sudo cp httpd.conf httpd.conf.`d`
$ sudo cp httpd.conf httpd.conf.$(d)
$ sudo cp httpd.conf !#.$(d)
$ sudo cp httpd.conf{,.$(d)}
$ ls -1 httpd.conf*
httpd.conf
httpd.conf.2014-04-08
```

Overwrite the Contents of a File

```
$ command > file
```

You can redirect output from one command to a file using the greater-than symbol. A single greater-than symbol (>) redirects standard output to a file, overwriting (truncating) any existing contents of the file. If no file exists, it creates one.

```
$ grep bash /etc/passwd > users-that-use-bash
$ cat users-that-use-bash
root:x:0:0:root:/root:/bin/bash
jason:x:501:501:Jason:/home/jason:/bin/bash
oracle:x:1006:1006::/home/oracle:/bin/bash
bob:x:1000:1000:Bob Smith:/home/bob:/bin/bash
$
```

Empty a File That Is Being Written To

```
$ > file
$ cat /dev/null > file
```

To quickly zero out a file you can redirect nothing to it. Why not just delete the file and recreate it? If a process has a file open when you delete it, the process will keep the file handle open and continue writing to that file. Only when the process closes the file handle will the disk space used by that file be freed. If an application fills up /var and you delete the open log file, /var will still be full. If you redirect nothing to the file, the file is truncated and the application can continue writing to the file.

```
$ sudo -s
# > /var/log/maillog
# ls -l maillog
-rw-------. 1 root root 0 Apr  9 18:55 maillog
```

Append a String to a File

```
$ command >> file
```

The double greater than sign (>>) redirects standard output to a file and appends to any existing contents. If no file exists, it creates one.

```
$ echo build new server >> todo.txt
$ cat todo.txt
build new server
$ echo add server to the load balancer >> todo.txt
$ cat todo.txt
build new server
add server to the load balancer
$
```

Follow a File as It Grows

```
$ tail -f file
```

For a file that is constantly being update like a log file, use tail -f to view the updates to the file in real time.

```
$ tail -f /var/log/syslog
Apr 10 21:45:01 linwww1 CRON[31769]: (root) CMD
(command -v debian-sa1 > /dev/null && debian-sa1 1 1)

Apr 10 21:46:28 linwww1 whoopsie[1421]: online

Apr 10 21:47:37  whoopsie[1421]: last message
repeated 2 times

Apr 10 21:55:01 linwww1 CRON[32548]: (root) CMD
(command -v debian-sa1 > /dev/null && debian-sa1 1 1)

Apr 10 22:05:01 linwww1 CRON[931]: (root) CMD
(command -v debian-sa1 > /dev/null && debian-sa1 1 1)

Apr 10 22:15:01 linwww1 CRON[2459]: (root) CMD
(command -v debian-sa1 > /dev/null && debian-sa1 1 1)

Apr 10 22:17:01 linwww1 CRON[2609]: (root) CMD (    cd
/ && run-parts --report /etc/cron.hourly)

Apr 10 22:25:01 linwww1 CRON[3197]: (root) CMD
(command -v debian-sa1 > /dev/null && debian-sa1 1 1)

Apr 10 22:35:01 linwww1 CRON[4036]: (root) CMD
(command -v debian-sa1 > /dev/null && debian-sa1 1 1)

Apr 10 22:35:33 linwww1 whoopsie[1421]: online
```

Watch Multiple Log Files at the Same Time

```
$ multitail file1 fileN
$ multitail file1 -I fileN
```

The multitail command allows you to browse through several files at once. Not only does multitail allow you to watch multiple files, it supports color highlighting, filtering, merging, and more. Here is a quick rundown of some of the most helpfuls commands for multitail.

F1 - Help
a - Add another file to follow
d - Delete a file from the view
/ - Start a search (Find)
ctrl-g - Exit a command, menu, or action. Similar to the emacs ctrl-g key binding.
q - Quit

```
$ sudo multitail /var/log/syslog  /var/log/kern.log

Apr 19 12:43:29 linuxsvr NetworkManager[758]: <info>
(eth0): IP6 addrconf timed out or failed.

Apr 19 12:43:29 linuxsvr NetworkManager[758]: <info>
Activation (eth0) Stage 4 of 5 (IPv6 Configure
Timeout) scheduled...

Apr 19 12:43:29 linuxsvr NetworkManager[758]: <info>
Activation (eth0) Stage 4 of 5 (IPv6 Configure
Timeout) started...

Apr 19 12:43:29 linuxsvr NetworkManager[758]: <info>
Activation (eth0) Stage 4 of 5 (IPv6 Configure
Timeout) complete.

00] /var/log/syslog *Press F1/<CTRL>+<h> for help*
132KB - 2014/04/19 12:46:45

Apr 19 12:43:08 linuxsvr kernel: [   10.012891]
Console: switching to colour frame buffer device
240x67

Apr 19 12:43:08 linuxsvr kernel: [   10.012926] fb0:
VESA VGA frame buffer device

Apr 19 12:43:11 linuxsvr kernel: [   12.288420] hda-
intel: Invalid position buffer, using LPIB read
```

method instead.

Apr 19 12:43:17 linuxsvr kernel: [18.891011] hda-intel: IRQ timing workaround is activated for card #0. Suggest a bigger bdl_pos_adj.

01] /var/log/kern.log *Press F1/<CTRL>+<h> for help* 132KB - 2014/04/19 12:46:45

To merge multiple files into one window, use the "-I" option. This intermixes the output of both of the files. This can aid in troubleshooting a problem.

$ sudo multitail /var/log/syslog -I /var/log/kern.log

Apr 19 12:43:08 linuxsvr kernel: [10.012891] Console: switching to colour frame buffer device 240x67

Apr 19 12:43:08 linuxsvr kernel: [10.012926] fb0: VESA VGA frame buffer device

Apr 19 12:43:11 linuxsvr kernel: [12.288420] hda-intel: Invalid position buffer, using LPIB read method instead.

Apr 19 12:43:17 linuxsvr kernel: [18.891011] hda-intel: IRQ timing workaround is activated for card #0. Suggest a bigger bdl_pos_adj.

Apr 19 12:43:29 linuxsvr NetworkManager[758]: <info> Activation (eth0) Stage 4 of 5 (IPv6 Configure Timeout) complete.

Apr 19 12:43:29 linuxsvr NetworkManager[758]: <info> Activation (eth0) Stage 4 of 5 (IPv6 Configure Timeout) scheduled...

Apr 19 12:43:29 linuxsvr NetworkManager[758]: <info> Activation (eth0) Stage 4 of 5 (IPv6 Configure Timeout) started...

Apr 19 12:43:29 linuxsvr NetworkManager[758]: <info> (eth0): IP6 addrconf timed out or failed.

```
00] /var/log/syslog *Press F1/<CTRL>+<h> for help*
132KB - 2014/04/19 12:48:32
```

Delete Empty Directories

```
$ find . -type d -empty -delete
```

If you ever find yourself needing to clean up empty directories, find can make that task a snap. Use the -type d option to find all the directories with the -empty option to only include empty directories and finally the -delete option removes the directories.

```
$ mkdir -p testing/{1..4}
$ ls testing/
1  2  3  4
$ find . -type d -empty -delete
$ ls testing/
ls: cannot access testing/: No such file or directory
$
```

Print a List of Files That Contain a given String

```
$ grep -rl string .
```

To get a list of files that contain a given string, use grep with the -r (recursive) and -l (list files that match) options.

```
$ sudo grep -lr jim /var/log
/var/log/audit/audit.log.1
/var/log/secure-20140406
/var/log/secure
```

An Easy-to-Read Recursive File Listing

```
$ find . -type f -ls
```

The ls command has a recursive option, but I find reading the output from the find command to be easier to digest, especially for a large number of files and directories. The advantage to using find is that it displays the full path to each file, unlike ls.

```
$ ls -lR Music/
Music/:
total 4
drwxr-xr-x. 2 jason jason 4096 Feb 22 12:40 jazz
Music/jazz:
total 20932
-rw-r--r--. 1 jason jason      79496 Feb 22 12:40
giant-steps.mp3
-rw-r--r--. 1 jason jason 21267371 Feb 16 11:12 jazz-
album-1.mp3
-rw-r--r--. 1 jason jason      79496 Feb  3 18:13
john-coletrane.mp3
$ find Music/ -type f -ls
397966 20772 -rw-r--r--  1 jason jason 21267371 Feb
16 11:12 Music/jazz/jazz-album-1.mp3
396787    80 -rw-r--r--  1 jason jason   79496 Feb 22
12:40 Music/jazz/giant-steps.mp3
132464    80 -rw-r--r--  1 jason jason   79496 Feb  3
18:13 Music/jazz/john-coletrane.mp3
$
```

View Files and Directories in a Tree Format

```
$ tree
$ tree -d
$ tree -L number
```

The tree command displays files and directories in a tree like format. If you only want to see the directory structure, use the -d option. To limit the depth of the tree, use the -L option followed by a number.

```
$ tree Music/
Music/
└── jazz
            ├── giant-steps.mp3
            ├── jazz-album-1.mp3
            └── john-coletrane.mp3
1 directory, 3 files
$ tree -d Music/
Music/
└── jazz
1 directory
$ tree -d /var | head
/var
├── account
├── cache
|   ├── fontconfig
|   ├── gdm
|   |   ├── adminuser
|   |   └── jason
```

```
|      ├── hald
|      ├── ldconfig
|      ├── man
$ tree -dL 1 /var
/var
├── account
├── cache
├── crash
├── db
├── empty
├── ftp
├── games
├── gdm
├── lib
├── local
├── lock
├── log
├── mail -> spool/mail
├── nis
├── opt
├── preserve
├── run
├── spool
├── tmp
├── www
└── yp
$
```

Replace a String in Multiple Files

```
$ find /path -type f -exec sed -i.bak
's/string/replacement/g' {} \;
```

If you have some information that is embedded in multiple files and you need to change it, use the find command in combination with sed. The -i option for sed tells it to perform an in-place edit. You can supply an extension to -i to create a backup of the file before the edits are made. The command passed to sed tells it to substitute "replacement" for "string" globally. A global substitution will perform the replacement everywhere. A normal substitution replaces only the first occurrence on a line.

In this example the server that houses software repositories is being replaced. With the following one-liner, all occurrences of "thor" are replaced by "loki."

```
$ grep -r thor .
./deploy-il.sh:REPO_SERVER="thor.company.com"
./deploy-ca.sh:REPO_SERVER="thor.company.com"
./deploy-fl.sh:REPO_SERVER="thor.company.com"
./deploy-ny.sh:REPO_SERVER="thor.company.com"

$ find . -type f -exec sed -i.bak 's/thor/loki/g' {} \;
$ grep -r thor .
./deploy-fl.sh.bak:REPO_SERVER="thor.company.com"
./deploy-il.sh.bak:REPO_SERVER="thor.company.com"
./deploy-ny.sh.bak:REPO_SERVER="thor.company.com"
./deploy-ca.sh.bak:REPO_SERVER="thor.company.com"
```

```
$ grep -r loki .
./deploy-il.sh:REPO_SERVER="loki.company.com"
./deploy-ca.sh:REPO_SERVER="loki.company.com"
./deploy-fl.sh:REPO_SERVER="loki.company.com"
./deploy-ny.sh:REPO_SERVER="loki.company.com"
$
```

Extract the Nth Line from a File

```
$ awk 'NR==N'
```

To extract a specific line from a file, tell awk to print the line that matches the line number. One area where this comes in helpful is when you encounter an error in a script. To see exactly what the script is doing on that line, use awk.

```
$ ./deploy.sh
./deploy.sh: line 74: /usr/local/bin/patch: No such
file or directory
$ awk 'NR==74' deploy.sh
/usr/local/bin/patch $NEW_HOST
$
```

Convert Text Files from Windows Format to Linux Format and Vice-Versa

```
$ dos2unix
$ unix2dos
```

Sooner or later you're going to be sent a file or download one that uses a pair of CR (carriage return) and LF (line feed) characters to terminate lines in the file. Those type of files are Windows/DOS formatted. Unix-like operating systems simply use the LF character to terminate a line. Sometimes this can cause issues. To convert the file to a unix-like format, use dos2unix. To examine the line termination characters use "cat -A" or the "file" command.

```
$ cat -A from-my-windows-buddy.pl
#!/usr/bin/perl^M$
print "This is a cross-platform perl script!\n"^M$
$ ./from-my-windows-buddy.pl
-bash: ./from-my-windows-buddy.pl: /usr/bin/perl^M:
bad interpreter: No such file or directory
$ dos2unix from-my-windows-buddy.pl
dos2unix: converting file from-my-windows-buddy.pl to
UNIX format ...
$ cat -A from-my-windows-buddy.pl
#!/usr/bin/perl$
print "This is a cross-platform perl script!\n"$
$ ./from-my-windows-buddy.pl
This is a cross-platform perl script!
$ file other-file.txt
other-file.txt: ASCII text, with CRLF line
terminators
$ dos2unix other-file.txt
dos2unix: converting file other-file.txt to UNIX
format ...
$ file other-file.txt
other-file.txt: ASCII text
$
```

The opposite side of this coin is that if you send a file created on a Linux host to someone who opens it in Notepad on Windows, they will see just one long line of text. Convert the file to Windows/DOS format with the unix2dos command.

```
$ file report-for-ceo.txt
report-for-ceo.txt: ASCII text
$ unix2dos report-for-ceo.txt
unix2dos: converting file report-for-ceo.txt to DOS
format ...
$ file report-for-ceo.txt
report-for-ceo.txt: ASCII text, with CRLF line
terminators
$
```

MISCELLANEOUS

Change to the Previous Working Directory

```
$ cd -
```

If you want to return your previous working directory, use "cd -". The OLDPWD environment variable holds the path of your most recent directory location. "cd -" is the same as "cd $OLDPWD".

```
$ cd /etc/httpd/conf.d
$ grep ^SSLCert ssl.conf
SSLCertificateFile /etc/pki/tls/certs/localhost.crt
SSLCertificateKeyFile
/etc/pki/tls/private/localhost.key
$ cd /etc/pki/tls/certs/
$ ls
ca-bundle.crt  ca-bundle.trust.crt  localhost.crt
make-dummy-cert  Makefile  renew-dummy-cert
$ cd -
/etc/httpd/conf.d
```

```
$
```

Reset Your Terminal Emulator Display

```
$ reset
```

Displaying binary files to your screen can cause your terminal to become unusable. To attempt to recover, type "reset" and press enter. Your terminal may be in such a state that you won't be able to see what you're typing, but you shell will still accept the input.

```
$ cat blue-train.mp3
F□□□A□□□□□□h□reset
$
```

Search Wikipedia from the Command Line

```
$ dig +short txt <string>.wp.dg.cx
$ host -t txt <string>.wp.dg.cx
```

If you need to quickly look up some information on a subject, you can search wikipedia using DNS. The name server returns wikipedia article summaries as TXT records.

```
$ dig +short txt linux.wp.dg.cx
"Linux is a Unix-like computer operating system
assembled under the model of free and open source
software development and distribution. The defining
component of Linux is the Linux kernel, an operating
system kernel first released 5 October 1991 by Linus
Torvalds. http://en.wikipedia.org/wiki/Linux"
$ host -t txt bash_shell.wp.dg.cx
bash_shell.wp.dg.cx descriptive text "Bash is a Unix
```

shell written by Brian Fox for the GNU Project as a free software replacement for the Bourne shell (sh).Bash is a command processor, typically run in a text window, allowing the user to type commands which cause actions. Bash can also read commands from a file, called a script. Like all Unix shells, it supports filename wildcarding, piping, here documents...
http://en.wikipedia.org/wiki/Bash_(Unix_shell)"

You can create a small shell script to save yourself from typing the full DNS query each time.

```
$ echo -e '#!/bin/bash\ndig +short txt ${1}.wp.dg.cx'
> wikidig

$ chmod 755 !$

chmod 755 wikidig

$ ./wikidig ubuntu_operating_system
```

"Ubuntu As of 2012, according to online surveys, Ubuntu is the most popular Linux distribution on desktop/laptop personal computers, and most Ubuntu coverage focuses on its use in that market. However, it is also popular on servers and for cloud computing.
http://en.wikipedia.org/wiki/Ubuntu_(operating_system)"

Alternatively, you could create a function instead and add it to your dot files.

```
$ echo 'wikidig() { dig +short txt ${1}.wp.dg.cx; }'
>> .bash_profile

$ . ~/.bash_profile
```

```
$ wikidig jazz

"Jazz is a musical style that originated at the
beginning of the 20th century in black communities in
the Southern United States. It was born out of a mix
of African and European music traditions. Its African
pedigree is evident in its use of blue notes,
improvisation, polyrhythms, syncopation and the swung
note. From its early development until the present
day jazz has also...
http://en.wikipedia.org/wiki/Jazz"
```

Make Non-Interactive Shell Sessions Behave the Same as Interactive Sessions

Make any customizations in ~/.bashrc. The contents of ~/.bash_profile:

```
if [ -f ~/.bashrc ]; then

source ~/.bashrc

fi
```

The shell behaves in slightly different ways when you log on interactively versus when you just connect to run a single command. The contents of .profile or .bash_profile are only executed for interactive sessions. If you are not aware of this subtle difference it may leave you scratching your head as to why something works perfectly when you log in and execute a command versus when you just ssh in to run that same command. You can save yourself some hassle by making your interactive and non-interactive sessions behave the same. To do this, configure .bash_profile to reference .bashrc and put all of your configuration in .bashrc.

Here is an example to better illustrate the difference between interactive and non-interactive shells. For example, if you define an alias for ll in ~/.bash_profile it will work during an interactive session but it will not be available during a non-interactive session.

Interactive:

```
mac:~ jason $ ssh linuxserver
jason@linuxserver:~$ uptime
 11:49:16 up 97 days,  2:59,  5 users,  load average:
0.15, 0.25, 0.31
jason@linuxserver:~$ ll
-rw-r--r-- 1 jason jason 221 Nov 13 11:30 file.txt
jason@linuxserver:~$ exit
logout
Connection to 10.0.1.9 closed.
mac:~ jason $
```

Non interactive:

```
mac:~ jason$ ssh linuxserver uptime
 11:49:16 up 97 days,  2:59,  5 users,  load average:
0.15, 0.25, 0.31
mac:~ jason$ ssh linuxserver ll
bash: ll: command not found
mac:~ jason$
```

```
$ cat .bash_profile
# Put our settings in .bashrc so we have the same
environment for login and non-login shells.
if [ -f ~/.bashrc ]; then
    source ~/.bashrc
```

```
fi
$ cat .bashrc
alias ll='ls -l'
HISTFILESIZE=5000
export HISTFILESIZE
```

Make Your Computer to Talk to You

```
$ espeak -f file
$ echo text | espeak
```

Espeak converts text to speech. You can provide espeak a file or pipe in text for it to speak. If you have a long running task you can let your computer tell you when it's finished as in this example.

```
$ for VIDEO in $(ls *.mp4 | sed 's/.mp4//')
> do
>   avconv -v quiet -i $x.mp4 $x.mp3
>done ; echo "File conversions complete." | espeak
```

Display the Current Date and Time
in a Different Time Zone

```
$ TZ=<TIMEZONE> date
```

The TZ environment variable specifies the time zone. If you want to know the time in a given time zone, prepend the environment variable and time zone to the date command.

```
$ TZ=America/Los_Angeles date
Sun Apr  6 19:37:46 PDT 2014
$ TZ=MST date
```

```
Sun Apr   6 19:37:48 MST 2014
$ TZ=CST date
Mon Apr   7 02:37:50 CST 2014
$ TZ=UTC date
Mon Apr   7 02:37:53 UTC 2014
```

It's a common practice to use UTC as the time zone on servers. If your workstation or laptop is set to a different time zone, you can create an alias that quickly gives you the time in UTC.

```
$ alias utc='TZ=UTC date'
$ utc
Mon Apr   7 02:35:01 UTC 2014
```

Display a Calendar at the Command Line

```
$ cal
$ cal MM YYYY
$ cal YYYY
```

To display an calendar at the command line use the cal command. Use the -3 option to display the previous, current, and next month. If you want to see the calendar for an specific month use MM YYYY or for an entire year use YYYY.

```
$ cal
      April 2014
Su Mo Tu We Th Fr Sa
       1  2  3  4  5
 6  7  8  9 10 11 12
13 14 15 16 17 18 19
20 21 22 23 24 25 26
27 28 29 30
$ cal -3
     March 2014            April 2014            May 2014
Su Mo Tu We Th Fr Sa  Su Mo Tu We Th Fr Sa  Su Mo Tu We Th Fr Sa
                  1         1  2  3  4  5               1  2  3
 2  3  4  5  6  7  8   6  7  8  9 10 11 12   4  5  6  7  8  9 10
 9 10 11 12 13 14 15  13 14 15 16 17 18 19  11 12 13 14 15 16 17
16 17 18 19 20 21 22  20 21 22 23 24 25 26  18 19 20 21 22 23 24
23 24 25 26 27 28 29  27 28 29 30           25 26 27 28 29 30 31
30 31
$ 10 2014
     October 2014
Su Mo Tu We Th Fr Sa
          1  2  3  4
 5  6  7  8  9 10 11
12 13 14 15 16 17 18
19 20 21 22 23 24 25
26 27 28 29 30 31
```

Extract a Tar Archive to a Different Directory

```
$ tar tarfile.tar -C /path/to/directory
```

Instead of changing directories and untarring a file, you can use the -C option.

```
$ tar xf projectfiles.tar -C /usr/local/myproject
```

This is equivalent to these two commands.

```
$ cd /usr/local/myproject
$ tar xf ~/projectfiles.tar
```

Transform the Directory Structure of a Tar File When Extracting It

```
$ tar xf tarfile.tar --strip-components=NUMBER
```

If you want to extract a tar file starting at a subdirectory, use the --strip-components option. For example, if you download a release from github.com the name and version of the project is the top directory in the tar file. To extract the files below that directory use --strip-components=1.

```
$ curl -sLO
https://github.com/twbs/bootstrap/archive/v3.1.1.tar.gz
$ tar ztvf v3.1.1.tar.gz  | head -1
drwxrwxr-x root/root           0 2014-02-13 12:24
bootstrap-3.1.
$  tar zxvf v3.1.1.tar.gz  --strip-components=1 -C
~/bootstrap-latest
$ ls -1 ~/bootstrap-latest
bower.json
```

```
CNAME
composer.json
_config.yml
CONTRIBUTING.md
dist
docs
fonts
grunt
Gruntfile.js
js
less
LICENSE
package.json
README.md
test-infra
```

Use a Spreadsheet from the Command Line

```
$ sc
```

If you're the kind of person that tries to do absolutely everything at the command line, then you'll like the spreadsheet calculator, SC. Also, if you're comfortable with vi, then sc will come naturally to you. In addition to using the arrow keys for navigation you can use the familiar h, j, k, and l keys. Like vi, g represents go. To go the cell D4 type gD4.

To enter a number or a formula navigate to the cell you want to edit and use = followed by the number or formula. To enter left justified text use the less-than sign (<) and the greater-than sign (>) for right justified text. To edit a cell type e. To save a file, press P followed by a filename. For quick help type ? and to quit, type q. For more information check out the tutorial that ships with SC.

```
$ sc
A2 (10 2 0) [@sum(A0:A1)]
                 A              B              C
   0            1.00
   1            3.00
   2            4.00
$ sc /usr/share/doc/sc/tutorial.sc
```

Rudimentary Command Line Stopwatch

```
$ time read
```

This command will stop when you press enter and display how much time elapsed. The real row contains the elapsed time.

```
$ time read
real      0m8.047s
user      0m0.000s
sys       0m0.000s
$
```

Repeat a Command at Regular Intervals and Watch Its Changing Output

```
$ watch command
```

If you want to monitor the output of a command, use watch. Watch will execute a command periodically and display its output. You can control the interval that the command is repeated by supplying a number of seconds to the -n option. This is great tool to watch processes, disk usage, number of logged in users, queue depths, etc.

```
$ sudo /usr/local/bin/compress-log-files &
[1] 15650
$ watch df -h /var
Filesystem                     Size  Used Avail
Use% Mounted on
/dev/mapper/vg_livecd-lv_root   28G  3.7G   24G  14%
/

...

Filesystem                     Size  Used Avail
Use% Mounted on
/dev/mapper/vg_livecd-lv_root   28G  3.3G   25G  12%
/
$ watch -n 1 "ps -ef| grep httpd | grep -v grep | wc
-l"
9
...
14
...
29
...
27
$
```

Execute a Command at a given Time

```
$ echo "command" | at time
$ at -f file time
```

If you ever need to reboot a server at midnight, but don't feel like staying up that late, schedule it with the at command. Actually you can schedule any command or set of commands that you need to run once at a given time with at. To list your at jobs use atq. Here's the reboot example.

```
$ sudo -s
# echo 'reboot' | at midnight
# atq
1    2014-04-13 00:00 a root
# exit
$ exit
```

You can provide at with a series of commands in a file by using the -f option. For example, you could send your boss a report at 5:00 PM on Friday and leave early to play a round of golf. If your conscience gets the better of you, you can delete your at job with atrm.

```
$ at -f email-tps-report-to-boss 5:00pm friday
job 2 at 2014-04-18 17:00
$ atrm 2
$ atq
$
```

Share Your Screen Session with Another User

```
$ screen -x user/session
```

In order to use multi user support for screen, the screen executable needs to be setuid for root.

```
$ sudo chmod u+s /usr/bin/screen
```

One user must start a screen session. It can be helpful to name your screen sessions with the -S option. To enable multi user session, type ctrl-a followed by ":multiuser on<enter>". To allow someone to connect to your session type ctrl-a followed by ":acladd username". To disconnect the other user from the screen session type ctrl-a followed by ":acldel username".

```
[jason@linuxsvr ~]$ screen -S for-bob
ctrl-a :multiuser on
Multiuser mode enabled
ctrl-a :acladd bob
```

When the other use is ready to connect to the screen session, they type screen -x followed by the session identifier. They can connect by PID or by name. IE, screen -x 1234 or screen -x session-name. When they are ready to disconnect, they can leave the screen session like any other by typing ctrl-a d. While the session is shared both parties not only can they see the same screen, but they both provide input by typing.

```
bob@linuxsvr:~$ screen -ls jason/
There is a suitable screen on:
        5428.for-bob        (Multi, attached)
1 Socket in /var/run/screen/S-jason.
bob@linuxsvr:~$ screen -x jason/for-bob
```

```
[jason@linuxsvr ~]$
ctrl-a d
[detached]
bob@linuxsvr:~$
```

Execute an Unaliased Version of an Aliased Command

```
$ \aliased-command
```

Use the escape character to ignore an alias for a command. For example, if "ls" is aliased to "ls -F", use "\ls" to execute "ls" without the "-F" option. The "-F" option to ls appends a file type indicator. In the case of directories that indicator is a forward slash (/).

```
$ alias ls
alias ls='ls -F'
$ ls
Desktop/  Documents/  Downloads/  examples.desktop
$ \ls
Desktop  Documents  Downloads  examples.desktop
$
```

Save the Output of a Command as an Image

```
$ command | convert label:@- image.png
```

To capture the output of a command in an image file, use the convert command from the ImageMagick software suite. If you want to email a password to someone, but don't want it travel around the Internet in plain text, put it in an image. When supplying the at sign (@) to label it tells convert to read input from the file following the at sign. The dash says the "file" is coming from standard input. If you want to create a simple image with some text you can supply a string to label.

```
$ echo "bob:changeme" | sudo chpasswd
$ echo "bob:changeme" | convert label:@- password.png
$ convert label:"bob:changeme" same-thing-different-way.png
$ echo "Here's your password.  Again." | mail -a
passwd.png -s 'Password reset' bob@mycompany.com
$
```

ABOUT THE AUTHOR

Jason Cannon started his career as a Unix and Linux System Engineer in 1999. Since that time he has utilized his Linux skills at companies such as Xerox, UPS, Hewlett-Packard, and Amazon.com. Additionally, he has acted as a technical consultant and independent contractor for small to medium businesses.

Jason has professional experience with CentOS, RedHat Enterprise Linux, SUSE Linux Enterprise Server, and Ubuntu. He has used several Linux distributions on personal projects including Debian, Slackware, CrunchBang, and others. In addition to Linux, Jason has experience supporting proprietary Unix operating systems including AIX, HP-UX, and Solaris.

He enjoys teaching others how to use and exploit the power of the Linux operating system and teaches online video training courses at http://www.LinuxTrainingAcademy.com.

Jason is also the author of *Linux for Beginners: An Introduction to the Linux Operating System and Command Line.*

INDEX

echo

espeak

exit

file

find

for

firefox

fusermount

getconf

grep

head

APPENDIX

Trademarks

Firefox is a registered trademark of the Mozilla Foundation.

ImageMagick is a registered trademark of ImageMagick Studio LLC.

Linux® is the registered trademark of Linus Torvalds in the U.S. and other countries.

Mac and OS X are trademarks of Apple Inc., registered in the U.S. and other countries.

Open Source is a registered certification mark of Open Source Initiative.

Sun and Oracle Solaris are trademarks or registered trademarks of Oracle Corporatoin and/or its affiliates in the United States and other countries.

UNIX is a registered trademark of The Open Group.

Windows is a registered trademark of Microsoft Corporation in the United States and other countries.

All other product names mentioned herein are the trademarks of their respective owners.

www.ingramcontent.com/pod-product-compliance
Lightning Source LLC
LaVergne TN
LVHW022335060326
832902LV00022B/4045